Kiss and Tell

Kiss and Tell

Tales by a Mother and Daughter

Stephanie Kay and Andi Kay

To order additional copies of this book, contact:
Xlibris Corporation
1-888-795-4274
www.Xlibris.com
Orders@Xlibris.com
53644

Contents

Chapter One

Dating

"Of course, you're nervous," your mother chuckled. "It's your first date!"

It was the Boy Scout dance.

You were twelve. He was thirteen.

He shifted from foot to foot and looked as if he'd give anything to be someplace else, as your parents chatted with him down in the hallway.

You came down the stairs in the dress your mother had assured you did not look as ugly as it had appeared in the mirror.

He looked at you in a way that made you certain it did.

"Hi," you said, pretending to smile.

"Hi," he replied, his voice an octave higher than usual.

"Have a good time!" your father shouted as you headed out the door.

* * *

"Nervous? Oh, c'mon," your teenage daughter said, rolling her eyes. "It's not like it's your first date. I mean, you and Dad dated, right?"

"Yes, but . . . we're talking more than twenty years ago." How, you wonder, could a forty-four-year-old mother of three possibly feel so much like a virgin? "I look awful in this outfit."

"Mom, you look great."

We both jumped as the doorbell rang.

"Hey, there he is," she said cheerfully, "I'll let him in!"

You paused, took a deep breath, told yourself the mirror was lying, and headed toward the front door.

He was shorter than he was supposed to be, with less hair, and looked at you in a way that makes you certain the mirror was not lying.

"Tom?" you said, tilting your head coquettishly and swaying a little off balance in the process.

He affirmed. "Hello!" He smiled, revealing an extraordinarily large gap between his two top front teeth.

"Have a good time!" your daughter shouted as you headed out the door.

*　　*　　*

Did you grow up thinking dating was something adolescents, teenagers, and college kids do? That it was a temporary activity that ended with meeting Mr. Perfect and marrying 'til death you did part?

Did you get a little impatient when Prince Charming still hadn't shown up by the time you were in your midtwenties?

Did you grow up in a world in which there were "spinsters"—single women over forty who knew, because of their advanced age, that all the men were taken, and they were destined to spend their remaining years alone?

Was being divorced relatively unusual? Was "widow" a tragic title a woman usually carried with her to the grave?

Have you, by any chance, been shocked to find your grown-up self—at age thirty-five, forty, forty-five, fifty, fifty-five, sixty, sixty-five, seventy, seventy-five, eighty (and beyond)—*DATING* again?

Well, welcome to the new demographics. Forty-four percent of adult Americans are single today, and in some areas of the country, the percentages are even higher. Fifty percent of the residents of New York State are single, for example, as are a whopping 70 percent of the adults in Washington, D.C. In terms of the nation as a whole, 100 million Americans are single today, more than the entire population of the United States in 1900!

Young people are marrying later, if at all. Marrieds are divorcing more often. Widowhood is no longer forever. The title "spinster" has been replaced by "swinging single," and just about *everybody* is "dating" (including some married people who pretend they're not married).

And, like everything else in our country, dating has become extremely high tech. There are hundreds of online dating services ready to match you up with someone close by or someone across the world. And for those looking for "someone exactly like me," there are also online dating services for Jews, Catholics, Protestants, Muslims, and all kinds of immigrant American groups—Indians, Pakistanis, Croatians, etc.

What has *not* changed, however, is the act of dating itself. Grown-up palms can get just as sweaty and clammy in terror of what is to come as those of a young girl on her first date. It doesn't matter whether you're seventeen or seventy; meeting someone for the first time means being judged. It conjures up feelings of discomfort, vulnerability, and self-consciousness even in the most confident professional women. *How do I look? How does he look? How do we look? What do I say? I can't believe I said that! Why am I feeling so fragile?*

It also brings out the irrational in perfectly rational people. You can spend the whole evening with a nonstop talker whose voice grates on you, someone you've decided is unattractive, uninteresting, and humorless to boot. Nonetheless, when, at the end of the evening, he announces that he's sorry, but you are simply not for him, you just might find yourself wondering what is wrong with *you*.

Dating is an experience you should not go through alone!

That's why we're here.

I married "forever," only to discover that forever was not to be when my husband of nineteen years, Stanley, died of cancer at age forty-four. I became a single parent of three teenagers. I got the professional credentials I needed to support a family and then did something I'd never thought I would be doing. I started dating! I met Richard and remarried. Six years later, I divorced Richard and began dating again. I have now been happily remarried to Lee for five years.

My daughter, Andi, decided to have a third child to save her failing ten-year marriage, only to find out that doing so caused her to grow farther apart from her husband, rather than closer together. When she realized things were not going to get better, she became a divorced mother of three . . . and a "dater". Andi has dated more than any of her friends because she refuses to become discouraged, even after some painful breakups. Her goal is to be part of a committed, loving relationship, and she is willing to put up with all the losers necessary in order to find that special man.

Mothers and daughters share clothes, jewelry, special moments, and secrets, but few in past generations have shared dating stories as single women. However, Andi and I both reemerged as singles at times in our lives when we least expected to do so, and between us, we have fifteen years of mature "dating" experience.

We have discovered—as we have compared notes over the years, soothed each other's egos, offered encouragement, and giggled uproariously over some of the funnier anecdotes our dating experiences have yielded—that commiseration can be both a learning and healing experience and—most important of all—great fun.

We broadened the circle to interview Andi's friends and my friends—two very different generations of dating women who shared with us as many unique stories about their experiences as there are dating services. We discovered we had all reached many similar conclusions, namely, that there are few problems that can't be rectified, that being a single parent makes dating difficult, but not impossible, that women are too hard on themselves in dealing with the opposite sex, that feeling lonely and sometimes depressed is par for the course, and that it's far better to laugh than to take these things too seriously.

Better yet, in addition to the stories, we had developed quite a body of expertise.

Our book is filled with our stories and newfound wisdom. It's a book that looks at dating from different generations, addressing some of the specific challenges each must face and advantages each has over the other. Younger women are usually more comfortable getting out there on the dating scene, for example, but older women tend to have a more solid sense of self.

We look at how children at home fit into the dating picture for younger women. (Is it possible to find a man who not only loves you but also adores your children? How much say should the children have in determining whether Mr. Perfect is perfect?) And we look at the discomfort older women might feel about suddenly dating again after forty plus years of marriage.

Ours is a book about two generations of women and all manners of men—too tall, too short, too fat, too skinny and just right; egomaniacs and caring partners; athletes and couch potatoes; knights in shining armor; and guys who wear their pants too high. It's also about guys who have psychological problems, yet try to pass themselves off as normal and their problems off on you.

This is a book about where to find them, when to keep them, why to break it off, and how to lose them. It's a book that tackles such important questions as: Should you fake orgasm? Is it okay to break up via voice mail? What if your kids don't like him? What if your kids like him and you don't? What secrets do body language convey? How do you spot a married man posing as a single? How do you read between the lines to know what's true and what's not? And what should you write in your online ad?

We fervently hope the following pages will enable all single women to learn what we've learned, laugh along with us at our mistakes, and thus have an easier time charting those uncharted waters on their way to new relationships.

Andi: I was a stay-at-home wife and a bit of a princess in my married life. When David and I separated, I had to reinvent myself big-time. I always enjoyed exercising, so I became certified as a personal trainer and have built up a flourishing business over the years. Who says princesses can't become competent adults? Don't think my life is a piece of cake; I still have to care for three children with all their appointments, bills, schoolwork, and activities. Sure I feel overwhelmed at times with everything on my plate, but I found that the key to functioning well is being organized. You need to decide what works for you, and we have lots of suggestions in our chapter on coping.

Stephanie: Nothing teaches you more about life's uncertainties than a husband's sudden death. Several years ago, I thought about writing a book which would be entitled *Living in the Gray*, a kind of a double entendre, about living life as an older woman and discovering that life is neither black nor white and can change at any moment. I've learned over the years not to fear change, but to embrace it. Think of uncertainties instead as surprises. Contemplate all you have in your life. Next, think about what you want. Third, think about how to get it. Then, think about what's stopping you. Can you do something about it? What kind of action can you take to change your situation? If you can't change your situation, think about ways to change your view of the situation. We'll cover that in our chapter on reframing.

Chapter Two

Starting Over

- Your marriage ended as a result of death or divorce.
- Your long-term partner broke up with you, or you broke up with him.

Whatever the reason and the result, you have experienced a major life change. You have struggled with the consequences and finally absorbed the new reality—grown from the experience, learned from it, healed from it, told your friends you've finally come to grips with it—and you are ready to take a stab at getting on with your life. You're ready to meet new people. You're ready to meet men, feel like a partner again, be less lonely, have some fun. You're ready to . . . start dating.

There is no one answer about the right time to start dating again. When Marcia started dating one month after her husband died, many people were critical; but she said she was very lonely, and it felt right to her. Cynthia, on the other hand, was so traumatized by her painful and lengthy divorce proceeding; she would not even think about dating until years afterward, when the scars had had time to heal.

The right time to begin dating is based on no one's time plan but yours. It's when you feel you're ready and reasonably comfortable.

Why Should I Date?

- It can be fun and exciting with the promise of a fabulous romance.
- It's nice to have someone to do things with. Sure, it's good to do things alone at times and know how to take care of yourself, but there's nothing like sharing a special moment with someone by your side. When you see a play you love or a movie you hate, don't you yearn to talk to someone about it?
- It's good to get a new perspective. Men have a very different view of parenting, dating, mating, and being single. It's helpful for women to hear this.
- It beats sitting home watching TV. Too many women claim exhaustion (and rightfully so) at the end of the day and are content (more or less) to escape in front of the TV. Preparing for a date may take more effort, but the result can be both energizing and stimulating.
- You can meet lots of interesting people, not only your new date but his friends as well. It's a great opportunity to expand your horizons.
- It expands your mind, too. If you're curious, you can learn something new from every person you go out with.
- It's a nice way to break the routine of work and kids and ease the loneliness of long empty nights.
- It helps you determine what it is you really want in a partner. It teaches you that everyone has faults, and it wouldn't hurt to become more tolerant. You may also learn how to compromise.

What You'll Need to Get Started

Let's start with an attitudinal change. Come out of that shell and expand your horizons in general. Regroup with old friends: invite people over, make lunch dates, and take steps to enlarge your circle. The more you socialize, the more social opportunities will come to you.

Get hip. Catch up with the times. Renew the newspaper and magazine subscriptions you let go during your too-depressed-to-bother period and get a grip on what's happening out there. This will prepare you for your future role as an interesting conversationalist and also give you some entertainment goals. What movie, play, art exhibit, and museum would you like to go see?

Make up that face! Look good all the time. Even the most insignificant errand could cause you to bump into someone you either know or might like to know.

Join a gym if you've let yourself go. Exercise will not only make you look better; it will make you feel so much better too. Health clubs are also excellent places to meet new people.

Update that ancient wardrobe of yours. Wear clothes that make you look good, rather than those you have a sentimental attachment to. You don't have to spend a fortune, but those pants from the eighties just have to go.

Remember, personal hygiene is about to become interpersonal. You may want to make an appointment to get your legs waxed. Married women can get lazy and let time elapse during the winter between leg shavings, but dating women can't. Single women need to reprioritize their daily living habits. Perhaps having electrolysis or laser hair removal would be a good move.

And then finally, (for the hope chest) new lingerie is a must. When was the last time you bought a sexy nightgown? When was the last time you bought attractive, rather than utilitarian, underwear?

Okay, now you're set to go.

Breaking the Ice

Stephanie: Ten months after my husband's death, I thought I would like to begin dating. My friends fixed me up with Jerry, a man they thought would make a good "teether" because he was kind and gentle. Was I nervous! I hadn't been with a man other than my husband Stanley for nineteen years! What should I wear? What would I talk about? What if he tried to get intimate?

Jerry turned out to be a perfect "teether." He was pleasant looking, easy to talk to, comfortable, rather than frightening, and we had a very nice evening. When he asked me how long I'd been dating, I looked at my watch and replied, "Thirty minutes." I felt good about holding my own in conversation. I asked him a lot of questions, and that made things easier. Most men enjoy talking about themselves and being genuinely listened to.

He asked me to take a walk on the beach the following day. I agreed, but the same characteristics that made him a comfortable first date made him dull as a second date. We had little left to say.

"Teethers" make that first step into the dating world easier, but when the molars grow in, it's time to move on!

Andi: What eased me into my new life as a single woman was socializing and going to dinners, movies, and parties with other single women my age.

About six months after my separation, I decided I was ready to get back into the dating game. I had not been on a date in thirteen years and couldn't believe how nervous I was. What should I wear? What should I talk about? Should I offer to pay for dinner? What was the protocol? What if he wanted to get intimate? My heart was pounding so loud that I could hear it!

I arrived first and decided to order a glass of wine while I waited. It calmed me down, and I was relaxed and ready when he arrived. I actually had a good time, and it really broke the ice. Even though we didn't see each other again, I had proven to myself that I could do this, and I was excited and optimistic to meet more potential prospects.

Taking Stock

Once you have gotten over the initial getting-back-to-dating-again jitters, you might want to pause and ask yourself some serious questions to help you navigate this social world a little more effectively.

- What are you looking for? Do you want an escort, someone who will take you to the social events you need to attend? Are you looking for a companion, a person with whom you can enjoy an occasional dinner and movie? Or, is your goal to develop a serious relationship?
- What characteristics (looks, personality, education, income, etc.) would a man have to have in order to appeal to you? Are these criteria realistic? Which are more important than others? How willing are you to look beyond superficial traits in order to give a date a chance?
- What are your deal breakers? We have known women who ended a potential relationship because of a man's political views. Others couldn't handle the religious differences. Which of these "deal breakers" listed by women we've interviewed would apply to you?

He keeps kosher. He's too religious, not religious enough, a vegan, a smoker, a loud chewer, a drinker, a nondrinker, a poor dresser, a drug user. He has bad breath, body odor, and bad manners. He is dating many women at the same time.

- What baggage might you be carrying? Are you a widow whose husband still looms too large in memory, making commitment to another impossible? Have you glamorized your ex, creating an image no man could equal? Has an ugly divorce made you distrustful of men in general? Are you still mourning an old relationship? Can you go into this with a positive attitude, an open mind, and a determination to make the most of the evening?

We have found that some women who were glad to be done with their marriages just want to enjoy the freedom for a while, while others want to start dating so they can "get it right this time."

After Eleanor was dumped by her spouse of fifteen years, she was anxious to go out and meet men. She quickly became involved with a man she was wildly attracted to, but he also dumped her, and then the reality set in. She thought if she jumped into a new relationship, she wouldn't have to deal with her husband's leaving. And here she was, faced with a double whammy.

She went into therapy and learned a lot about herself. After several months, she finally met someone she liked, and that terrified her. What did she do to protect herself? She went on a fault-finding mission, convincing herself he wasn't for her. Fortunately, he kept pursuing her, and she finally confronted her fears.

She is now ready to take the plunge and become intimate with him.

Dating Issues

It's never easy to start dating after a marriage ends, either by divorce or the death of a spouse. The longer you were married, the more you'll find the dating game has changed.

Who Pays for Dinner?

Marge had been with one man in her life—her high school sweetheart. After forty-five years of marriage, Len died. Marge was bereft and grieved for a long time. After a couple of years, she met Edward at a Widow/Widower Support group. Edward invited Marge out to dinner, and she accepted. She was a wreck. What should she wear? What should she talk about? How should she act? Should she let him walk her to the door? What if he tried to kiss her goodnight?

Marge heard that women sometimes split the bill, and when the check came, she didn't know what to do. Fortunately, Edward reached for the check as soon as it was put on the table.

It was quite a different ending with Suzanne and Nick. When the bill came, he picked it up, looked at it, and said, "Your share is $35.00, plus $8.50 for tax and tip."

Then there was Cathy, who offered to split the bill when it came, even though Ken had invited her for dinner. She was flabbergasted when he accepted. But no one was as cheap as Aaron, who met Andi at Starbucks. She ordered water. He had a latte and a scone, and when she offered to pay, he actually took the money!

What's the Right Thing to Do?

Generally, if the man called you and invited you to dinner, he should pay. If you met on one of the online dating services, you can offer to pay your share and see what happens. From what we've heard, when women offer to pay for the entire bill and men take them up on the offer, women generally don't want to see those guys again.

Some of the dating services have rules that each person should pay his or her own way, but some men still pick up the check, and that's always looked upon favorably. If he asks you to share the bill, you'll have to decide whether he has enough going for him to make you want to see him again and pay for the pleasure.

On the other hand, don't be a taker. If he takes you out a few times, you can either invite him for brunch or dinner, or pick up the tab. It's okay to be honest about how you feel. Many men appreciate the feedback.

What's Your Ideal Age Range?

Many people in the audience laughed uproariously during the scene in the movie *Must Love Dogs* when Diane Lane's character answers a personal ad from a very romantic-sounding man, only to discover, when she's seated at the appropriate table in the restaurant, that the mystery man who placed the personal ad is . . . her father!

What's funny in the movies is often less funny in real life. Carol, who became a widow at sixty, was appalled when she discovered her father, an eighty-five-year-old widower, told her he was "interested in dating a woman your age or even younger." "Why?" she wanted to know. "Because younger women make a man feel younger!" he replied.

He is not alone. It's an ego thing. Many men are looking for much younger women, which seriously cuts down on the availability of men for women in the over-fifty age group. Sylvia, who is sixty, reports that when a friend tried to fix her up with a seventy-three-year-old man, the man backed out, saying she was too old for him.

In truth, men who are searching for the fountain of youth by dating much younger women are probably too vain and superficial for any real relationship. A man truly comfortable with himself appreciates a woman who has more substance to offer than an attractive birth date.

But be prepared. This is a trend among older men.

Stephanie: It's so important for women of my generation to learn to value themselves as individuals. I remember being invited to a dinner party where I was the only single person and thinking that I had to be stimulating enough for two people. After a few times I noted that with many couples, generally only one of them had anything of interest to say anyhow. By bringing myself to the table, I decided finally, I was bringing enough!

If you don't value yourself as an individual, how can you expect someone else to value you?

Marlene was smart and attractive, but she had come out of a messy divorce with her self-esteem at an all-time low. She was introduced to a lovely man. She noticed that whenever he asked her to choose a restaurant, rather than choose what she enjoyed, she chose a moderately priced restaurant, even though he could easily afford a better one. This same man wanted to buy her a little gift for her birthday, even though they had only been dating a few weeks. She was uncomfortable accepting a gift at this point and politely declined. This seemed to be a pattern with her, and when she thought about it, she realized that she was sending a message about herself—that she wasn't worthy of gifts or expensive restaurants!

She had to practice saying "thanks" rather than "no thanks," and though it took her a while to work through this, she is feeling more positive about herself.

Andi: Starting over is difficult at any age. Younger women have a larger pool of men from whom to choose, but many of us have small children to worry about and very little free time. Finding free time was a real challenge for me. My life was very scheduled, and I was sensitive to being away from my children. When my ex-husband began taking the kids every other weekend and once during the week—the change was good for them and for me—it gave me the needed breather, the time to regenerate and go out without feeling guilty.

Dating By-Products

Friendships: We have had lots of good dates and lots of bad ones. It is important to go in with a positive attitude and reasonable expectations, so you won't be disappointed. Most Mr. Rights will probably turn out to be Mr. Wrongs instead. Just remember there's always someone new to meet, and even if you don't meet the man of your dreams, you may meet a perfectly nice guy who will turn out to be a friend. We have fixed up several men we knew with some of our friends. This has resulted in two marriages and one ongoing relationship. Don't burn your bridges. The singles circle is very small, and it's important to be nice to everyone.

Patience: One of our pet peeves is men not asking us questions. Early in Stephanie's dating career, she was fixed up with a man who talked about himself nonstop. When he finally asked her a question, she couldn't help but reply, "Do you know that's the first question you asked me since we've been here?" Now this confrontational position was during her early single days. She has since learned that it doesn't pay and only creates hard feelings.

A better response would be either to get through the evening and just say no to further invitations or give him an extra chance. We know that men communicate differently than women. You might try prompting him a little when he has shared an experience with you, by saying, "That's interesting. I had a similar experience." If, after you relate your experience, he doesn't follow up with questions or at least curiosity, chances are he's more interested in talking than listening.

Can he be trained? Probably, but is it worth your time and effort? Stephanie was able to train Arnie to ask questions, but only to her. He was invited to her home for brunch along with her cousin, Elaine. Elaine asked him several questions about his life, while he asked her none. Exasperated, Stephanie finally said to him, "And what do you want to know about Elaine?"

"What kind of bagel do you want?" he asked. Some men just aren't easy learners.

Patterns

Michael called Marybeth every Tuesday and Thursday. He would call on Tuesdays to make a date for the weekend, and he would call on Thursdays to just say hi and check in.

Sam called Alice every other day to check in. He would always make a date to see her again at the end of the previous date, so she knew he was interested. He was extremely attentive and respectful. But she also dated guys whom she had a great time with and then wouldn't hear from them for days or sometimes even weeks.

Everyone has patterns, and the earlier you learn what they are, the earlier you can know what to expect and whether this person will be a good prospect for you . . . or just a flaky, sporadic dater. Your expectations will be more realistic, and you won't have to wait by the phone or check your voice mail every five minutes.

Dos and Don'ts of Starting Out

Do

- Be a good listener. Pay attention to what he says.
- Prepare before your date. Read an interesting article that would make for a good discussion to get things going. Think of things you might want to ask him or tell him.
- Maintain your humor, even if things get a bit tense. Laughter does a lot to break up tension.
- Smile a lot and have positive body language. (Don't have your arms crossed, which shows you are in a defensive mode.)
- Have reasonable expectations—after all, it is just a first date.
- Try to enjoy yourself and have fun.
- Keep it light.
- Be prompt. Showing up late gets things off to the wrong start.
- Be polite to your restaurant server. We've been with men who treat servers like underlings, and it's a total turnoff.
- Keep your cell phone off.
- Be positive!

Don't

- Keep looking around to see who else is there, rather than giving him your undivided attention.
- Try to top his stories with one of your own. "You think that's something—wait till you hear what happened to me!" This will get you nowhere.

- Make a snap decision after greeting him at the door or at the restaurant table that he's not for you. That will get you in a negative mindset, when there may be gold beneath those ratty clothes!
- Get involved too quickly. It could lead to hurt and disappointment.
- Talk about your children. He wants to get to know you, not your kids. There will be plenty of time for that later, if you get to later.
- Talk about your ex. It's not only inappropriate but also a turnoff.
- Chew gum (talking about turnoffs!)
- Speak loudly—especially after having a couple of drinks
- Wear clothes that are too revealing or low cut.
- Bad-mouth other people, tempting though it may be.
- Drink too much. Many people become loose-tongued and loud, which is a turnoff not only for your date but for those sitting nearby as well.
- Order the most expensive thing on the menu. Take cues from what your date orders.
- Complain about your life. No one wants to hear it.
- Become sexually intimate immediately.
- Brag about yourself. A little humility goes a long way.

Chapter Three

Different Strokes for Different Folks

There are as many theories about why we choose the men we choose as there are potential partners. There's the nose theory, for example, that we pick our partners for life by their smell. Some experiments have found that men instinctively find women more attractive when they are near ovulation and, without realizing it, know instinctively when they are near ovulation by their odor, and that women's preferences for certain male features change, depending on what stage the women are in their menstrual cycle. This manner of choosing is, of course, entirely subconscious.

Another subconscious nose theory holds that we can sniff out genetic differences, that we are all instinctively looking for mates who possess genes that are compatible with our own in order to reproduce successfully and ward off pathogens in the next generation, and we somehow identify these people by the scent they give off. To avoid genetic inbreeding, the scientists say, we tend to pick partners whose smell is different from our own.

The nose theories offer a whole new dimension to the concept of "sexual chemistry" and might help answer often-whispered questions like, "What can she *possibly* see in *him*?" (Answer: It's not what she *sees* in him!)

Then there's the flab theory that our flesh is just as important as background, class, wealth, or age in determining whom we choose to spend the rest of our lives with; and thus we tend, subconsciously again, to choose mates who have a level of body fat that is similar to our own. Scientists think this could help explain the current national obesity epidemic.

And finally there's the visual theory. The statistics collectors say that men tend to desire women with features that suggest youth and fertility. Women, although they have strong preferences for male virility, often find themselves attracted to men who look as if they have wealth or the ability to acquire it.

While science is fascinated by the intrinsic and instinctive, the innate physical drives that pull human beings blindly and unconsciously to a member of the opposite sex, we nonscientists tend to place greater emphasis on rational choice.

The man that I'm looking for will be . . .

The woman I desire will have . . .

Rational choices too, however, often lead to dating patterns that appear irrational.

Take Michelle, for example. Michelle is forty years old, and she is dating a twenty-four-year-old bartender named Todd. She met him while she was out with friends and he was tending bar and considered him a fun summer fling. She ended up falling for him, even though she knew he wasn't for her in the long run.

She has two children, ages ten and eight.

Todd lives with his parents, doesn't want to do anything other than tend bar, and still receives an allowance from his mother!

What's the matter with Michelle?

It has taken Michelle a year to extricate herself from a disastrous marriage to an intense, psychologically sadistic man, and she is looking for distraction without strings. The last thing she feels she needs is to lock herself into another commitment right now. She happens to be in the mood for lighthearted fun and good sex.

Her friends tell her there is no future in this relationship.

She says, "Just as well!"

While some people date to mate, Michelle at this moment in her life just wants to date to date.

She's not alone. Amalie has been a single mom for years and intends to remain that way. While she enjoys adult companionship from time to time, she is highly spiritual and enjoys being alone. She also relishes having the kind of control over her own life she feels she can only maintain by living without a partner. "When I put my pen in a certain place, I know it's going to be right there when I come home, and I like that," she says.

Caroline, on the other hand, was married for ten years to a husband who left her and her daughter three years ago to marry another woman with children of her own. It was a devastating blow for Caroline, and she swore off men forever. Then she got lonely, so she began dating online. Recently, Caroline has fallen in love with someone who has neither been married before nor fathered children of his own and not only adores her, but adores her daughter too.

What is the point of all these anecdotes?

Everyone's story is unique. There are no one-size-fits-all answers when it comes to dating. It's so easy to compare ourselves to those who seem to have it all and bemoan our fate. Remember, however, that when it comes to other people's relationships, things are not necessarily as perfect as they seem.

More important, we are each looking for different things, and what we are looking for often changes from time to time as we ourselves change. The key is to figure out what we need to have a satisfying life—either with or without a mate—and pursue those needs.

Sheila thought Norman was a nice-looking, kind, and generous man who loved to do all the things she enjoyed doing. The only problem was that she wasn't physically attracted to him, and physical attraction was very important to her. She told herself how handsome he was and that she was being irrational, but the more she pushed herself, the more convinced she was that this would not work. She just couldn't pretend. When he invited her to New York for a weekend, she couldn't accept and decided it was time to end the relationship. Her friends told her she was crazy, that he was such a terrific catch; she was foolish to give up all the good things in the relationship just because the physical attraction wasn't there, but she just couldn't do it. Norman soon found another woman who fell in love with his many attributes, and he remarried long before Sheila did. Her friends offered sighs and I-told-you-so looks. Did she think something was wrong with her? Not at all, it just reinforced her belief that everyone has different needs and desires.

Some women enjoy dating younger men, while others prefer men who are closer to their age or older. For some, older represents stability and settling down, while for others, younger means good sex, fun, and excitement.

Know yourself. What do you want? Is dating a means to a desired end—finding a man with whom you can settle down happily for life—or do you view dating as an end in itself, a means of having an enjoyable social life?

What are you looking for? What characteristics are most important to you?

Looks: His eyes, hair color, height, weight, carriage, build?

Sex appeal: His chemistry, prowess, consideration, ability to please?

Personality: His wit, charm, generosity, kindness, thoughtfulness, boisterousness, shyness, conversational level?

Status: His intelligence, education, wealth, occupation, background, potential?

Age: Old and secure enough to take care of you? Young enough to be fun?

Common interests: Sharing your love for hiking, biking, music, politics, reading, tennis, golf, theater, surfing the Internet, or watching television?

Independence: Someone who lives alone and has neither psychological baggage, nor human baggage, like kids or nasty ex-partners?

Religion: Someone who shares your beliefs?

Moral qualities: With a history of fidelity, honesty, trustworthiness?

Other characteristics: You choose.

Think through this list and then rate the characteristics that are important to you in order of their importance. Which are the "gotta haves" and which are the "wanna haves"?

While it's important to understand your own personal desires, however, it's equally important to write this list in pencil, not ink. Dating, after all, is a growth experience; and as you date, you'll find yourself making all kinds of adjustments. Sometimes finding something we didn't even know we were missing changes everything.

Janet is a very attractive fifty-one-year-old woman who is in terrific shape, dresses smartly on a limited budget, and has a beautiful smile. She had dated several people since divorcing her philandering husband eight years earlier. Then her cousin offered to set her up with Paul, an extremely wealthy but very unattractive, overweight man who came from a large Italian family. Her cousin was up front. Paul was kind, he told her, but nothing in the looks department, and rumors had it that his family had mob connections. Janet agreed to meet him anyhow and, in fact, did find him evasive about his family's business. He was, just as had been described, overweight and unattractive. Yet, she continued to see him. Paul doted on Janet as no man ever had, wining and dining her, giving her expensive gifts, and taking her on exotic vacations. A year and a half after Janet started dating Paul, they became engaged. Her friends were shocked. "How on earth can she sleep with him every night?" they whispered. "How can she look at him?" Janet, however, seemed happier than she had ever been.

Was it love? Was it money? Was it the sheer fact that Janet spent a lot of time with Paul and grew to enjoy him? Studies show that if people spend a lot of time together, enjoy each other's company, and are kind to each other in the process, they can fall in love without checking off as "affirmative" a list of desirable characteristics. Before she met Paul, Janet would not have listed "unattractive, overweight man from Mafia-connected family" on her list of dating preferences! But then, she had never been indulged before. Sometimes what we think we want is very different from what we end up wanting.

And sometimes it helps to repeat the mantra, *different strokes for different folks.* This is a very personal decision, and one that should be made without paying unnecessary attention to the opinions of others, no matter how concerned they may be for your welfare.

Jacob introduced himself to Cindy at a singles dance. He was good looking, had an intriguing smile, and she was instantly attracted to him. He had been divorced for five years and had grown children. She had been divorced for nine years and also had grown children. Jacob was a CPA who turned out to live just around the block from her. She couldn't believe she had never met him before! They started dating and had great times together. They went to the theater, the opera, to interesting museums, and fabulous restaurants. When she found out that he had had two heart attacks in the past three years, she became concerned, but not concerned enough to stop dating him.

"He could have another heart attack and drop dead, or worse, end up an invalid with you taking care of him," her mother warned her. "Cut it off before you get into trouble!"

Cindy listened to her heart instead of her mother and married Jacob. They've now been married for three years and have enjoyed every day together. As far as Cindy is concerned, Jacob was well worth the risk.

Every set of circumstances is different. Some people shy away from becoming involved, while others plunge right in. Some never find the Prince Charming of their dreams but find true happiness instead with someone who fits in very well with their reality. Know your priorities, but leave yourself open to chance.

Dos and Don'ts of Different Strokes

Do

- Think about what you want at this stage of your life and pursue it.
- Try to put your best foot forward. Give it your all even though it isn't easy. Guys can sense when you are not that into it so try to be enthusiastic and positive.

Don't

- Compare yourself to your friends. What's good for them may not be good for you.
- Let your friends and family influence whom you date. If you are the type of person who is easily swayed, try listening to yourself instead.

Chapter Four

Coping Strategies for the Lean Times

- The man you've fallen in love with forgot to mention that he's married with three children.
- You're rejected by the too short, too old guy you only dated out of sympathy.
- Prince Charming confides that he can't stand your younger daughter.
- After dedicating almost a year to someone you were certain was "the one," you realize you've made a mistake.
- You are so sick of boring, self-absorbed, obnoxious men you never want to go out again.

Dating can add romance, excitement, and joy to your life. It can also be a source of self-doubt, rejection, and suffering, and nothing prompts such negative emotions more than the end of a long-term relationship. If you are the one to end the relationship, you may be upset about the amount of sadness your decision will create for someone else. That upset pales, however, in comparison to the trauma you feel when you are on the receiving end of the bad news.

Many women react by running right out and trying to immerse themselves in someone new, someone who will either confirm the soundness of their decision to break up or prove to them that they are not losers.

Habits become comforting. It is difficult to find yourself alone after being accustomed to spending long periods of time with the same person. Thinking of yourself as single after feeling for so long like part of a couple can create an emptiness. If the relationship has been going on very long, chances are its termination feels more like a death than a breakup. There are suddenly empty spaces in your life to be filled, happy memories that now make you sad. If you rejected him, you might be feeling guilty. If he rejected you, the impact on your ego can be devastating.

Spending some time grieving over a lost relationship is a good way to learn from it. Try a little self-exploration—what worked, what didn't work, and why? Did you know he was not right from the start? Are you looking for the right characteristics in a man? What warning signs might you look out for in the future? What will you do differently next time? What did you learn about yourself from this experience?

You will probably experience sadness, loneliness, and depression. These are very normal feelings under the circumstances. There are no easy shortcuts here, no quick modes of escape. *You need to go through it in order to get through it.* More important, an introspective pause can be very useful. We tend to learn more about ourselves during painful times than during pleasurable ones, and that learning can serve us well in the future. Remember our old friend Nietzsche who told us "what doesn't kill us makes us stronger." (By now, some of us are *very* strong!)

Expand Your Interests

This might be a good time to try new things and to find and explore a new passion. Many women have reported that finding a new and satisfying activity puts them in a fresh place. It creates an energy that spills over to the psychological, physical, and spiritual areas of their lives, enabling them to feel more energized and look at the world in a more positive way.

Take a vacation. Zero in with more energy on your career, on a hobby, on activities with friends and family. Distract yourself. That way, if a man comes along, it's icing on an already-delicious cake. We have long felt that in order to be part of a relationship you have to be a fully functioning woman—not one who needs a man so she can feel complete.

Affirm Yourself

This is not the time to blame yourself. (*"If only I had been more considerate, more affectionate . . . brushed my teeth more often . . . If only I had ignored his eating habits, tedious anecdotes, body odor, disregard for my comfort, and distended gut."*)

Rather, this is the occasion to regroup, rethink your goals, and strengthen your belief in yourself as the valued and unique person you are.

Seek Refuge in Humor

Remembering little annoyances is always therapeutic because no matter how gorgeous, brilliant, and charming the guy who has dumped you appears after the dumping, there had to be some inconsequential quirk that you overlooked in order to better enjoy the big picture. To get your mind pumping, we offer some of our own petty peeves:

First, there was Mel, who was always late (except when he climaxed).

Then there was Phil who was so endlessly, tediously, proudly punctual you could set your clock by him—never a moment too soon or a second too late—right on the minute!

How about Lenny who drove so slowly that elderly drivers honked and snarled as they whizzed around him?

Or Arty, who was always sniffing. No, it wasn't cocaine, just a non-ending sinus problem.

There was Jimmy, whose untrimmed nose and ear hair was such a distraction you even contemplated trimming it while he was asleep! Not to mention those bushy eyebrows that went up over his left eye and down over his right.

Then there was "high-pockets" Herb whose physique and clothing choices made it difficult to tell where his waist ended and hips began.

And, of course, Charlie who always stuck his tongue out of the corner of his mouth when he was thinking.

Or Emmit, who took forty-five minutes to eat his breakfast because he loved to hear himself speak (and for some reason used the word "perhaps" in every other sentence).

And let's not forget John with the two-to-eight-second-interval nose twitch that seemed to get more frequent as he got excited.

Introverted Izzy was a great lover but couldn't carry on a conversation when there were more than two people present . . . unlike Izzy's diametrical opposite "Dominating Dan" who rarely let anyone else get a word in edgewise. Surely these examples can provoke some memories of your own and help bring even the most maudlin among us back to reality!

Revisit What Went Wrong

When was the turning point in this relationship, and who caused it?

If you were the dumper, should you have done it sooner? Did you continue a relationship you knew deep down was wrong for you, and if so, *why* did you do it?

If you are having second thoughts about terminating, force yourself to go back in time and remember exactly how you felt just before you decided to bail out. Were those totally justifiable reasons? How many of your misgivings are due to feeling lonely at this moment?

If you were the dumpee, remind yourself that nothing gets a person's unequivocal attention the way rejection does. But rather than play into the melodrama, answer a few questions honestly: Did he just beat you to the punch? Could you honestly have been happy with him? If you could choose from all the men in the world, would you have chosen him?

- Instead of saying, "What's wrong with me that made him stop calling," try changing your message to "I wonder what his issues are?"
- Probe a little. It is better and healthier at this moment to shift the focal point and take a long hard look at some of the unknowns:

1. Might he have another girlfriend?
2. Is he commitment phobic?
3. Is he incapable of having a long-term relationship?
4. Does he have sexual issues?
5. Is he self-centered?
6. Is this part of a pattern?
7. Is he thoughtful?

8. Were there clues you should have picked up in the way he talked about his relationships with other women?

Below are some real-life examples with which you might identify.

Andi: Larry not only talked about other current relationships but also showed me pictures of some sexy young women he had dated. Was he trying to make me jealous or was he totally insecure? I decided it was both and stopped seeing him.

Stephanie: When Earl broke up with me, he said his new job would require constant travel, and he couldn't commit to a relationship. I was surprised and disappointed because we had such a good time together and had been seeing each other for several months. Then I heard he had prostate cancer and chose to handle it alone.

If You Can't Change It, Reframe It

Stephanie: When I used to visit my mother who had Alzheimer's disease, I learned to be a master "reframer." She no longer spoke, nor knew who I was. Gradually, I learned to view it as a good day if she opened her eyes and smiled at me. She may not have known who was hugging her, I told myself, but at least she knew someone was, and that made me feel better.

Reframing the situation after a horrendous dating experience involves counting up all the things you have to be thankful for—a satisfying career, perhaps, good friends, a strong support group, a great family, skills, hobbies, interests—and telling yourself that if the right man came along, that would be the cream in the coffee . . . but to tell the truth, you could continue to enjoy drinking it black.

You can reframe dates to make them more enjoyable, even dates with people you know are not for you. So you're not in love with the guy.

That doesn't mean he can't be an interesting companion, an entertaining conversationalist. So what if he has a double chin or an eye that goes in a funny direction? Reframe him as your ticket to eating in a restaurant you've always wanted, to try or going to that movie you've been wanting to see, or to initiating a fascinating discussion about world affairs.

Example: The moment Alan appeared at our agreed-upon meeting place at the symphony, I knew he was not for me. But he turned out to be a good-natured gentleman who enjoyed having fun. We did not fall in love, but we did enjoy dining at various ethnic restaurants, sharing a love for theater, and having interesting discussions.

Example: Donald was another of those not-for-me-in-the-long-term guys who was fun to be with now and then. We dated for over a year, during which time we traveled to interesting places, and he turned me into an enthusiastic opera fan.

No matter how bad the date, you can always learn something new! (How's that for a good reframe?) Try to live in the moment and look for some good in the person. Granted, sometimes it takes a lot of looking in order to enjoy the evening and even getting a little buzzed. If you ask a lot of questions, chances are you'll learn about an area or specialty you knew nothing about before. This always makes things more interesting—even if you know this will be your last date.

You can reframe rejection. When I started dating Eric, he looked so good on paper that I really wanted it to work. When he stopped calling after three dates, I suddenly remembered the garlic breath. There are always fatal flaws lurking in the shadows.

Another way to reframe rejection is to tell yourself the right person is somewhere out there, and this person just isn't the right person. Remind yourself how much you have accomplished in a few short years, and that you want someone who deserves you! (After telling yourself this several times, you will actually start to believe it.)

Repeat all your positive traits out loud while driving to work in the car and remind yourself of how strong you've grown. Stressing the positives and blocking any negative thoughts repeatedly will put you in a better place. It doesn't always happen instantly; sometimes you have to continue repeating your positive traits for a while, but it's a strategy that works.

Have you been on a run of dating dysfunctional men of late? Instead of stewing over your bad luck, sit back and contemplate how fortunate you are to be normal, stable, grounded, and hardworking, with a wonderful family and/or an amazing group of friends, both married and single. You are NOT dysfunctional. That's certainly something to celebrate!

You can reframe loneliness: Facing a weekend with no plans in sight? Reframe it as a "free" weekend, and you might actually begin to look forward to it. Tell yourself this is time that you deserve to relax and have no schedule after the hectic week you've just gone through. Catch up on your sleep. Browse through your favorite stores. Rent a fun movie. You just might end up wondering what you were so sad about.

Or if you want to translate an empty weekend into a busy one, make a schedule of "to do" items, such as organizing your closet, working out, doing errands. Take your time browsing through stores, working out leisurely, and best of all, catching up on your sleep. Before you know it, you'll have a fully booked weekend and feel good about accomplishing projects you'd been putting off.

Sometimes you just can't find a reframe for rejection: For example, Melinda had gone out only three times with a man she met on the Internet. Each time things seemed to be going well, but then he suddenly dumped her. Melinda had been dumped before and just couldn't find a suitable reframe. She couldn't stop feeling that something had to be wrong with her. (Rejection hurts. There's no getting around it. Repeated rejection hurts more.) Melinda was sad and depressed for a while, but gradually she began to feel better. She removed her name from the dating service, deciding to take a breather for a while. She treated herself to a massage and facial. She called single friends and went to dinner, art exhibits, theater, and movies. Gradually, she reminded herself that men were only one part of her life. The other parts were rich and fulfilling. By moving the dating life to the back burner for a while, she concentrated on all that was good in the other areas of her life, until she felt self-confident enough to try again.

Other Coping Skills

Selective ignoring. Ron had a mole on his nose that drove Eleanor crazy. No matter how she tried not to, she would always end up staring at this oversized mole. Yet, he was so nice to her, and they had so much in common. Was she going to let a good one get away because of an innocuous mole? She tried focusing on his eyes, and lo and behold, it worked. It's the same with personality issues. We've heard stories about men who talked about their kids or themselves too much, were too detailed, repeated stories, and did a host of other annoying things. But when all else is good, maybe you need to weigh how important these small flaws are in the greater scheme of things.

Can you learn to ignore them? If the good parts outweigh the bad, you may want to focus on all that's good. In time you will know if this is working for you.

Positive self-talk. Ruth had grown up in a family where criticism was the norm. If her mother wasn't there to criticize her, she could do a good job herself. "If I weren't so fat, ugly, dumb, etc., maybe people would like me," she said. Friends convinced her to go into therapy, and she was able to make some life-altering changes. First, she learned how to change the negative messages into affirmations. Every day she would look in the mirror and say, "I'm a terrific woman. I'm losing weight and looking so much better in my clothes. I'm intelligent, have a good career, and I'm attractive. I've been through tough times and survived. I'm a good friend whom people can depend on."

Ruth practiced these affirmations at least twice a day, and more if the critical Ruth started popping up. It really helped her. She kept a journal of all the nice things she had done each day, like smiling at a stranger or going out of her way for a friend. With time and a therapist's help, she was able to send the negative Ruth far away.

Laughter. Amy prayed the guy at the restaurant table wasn't the blind date she had arranged to meet. He was at least fifteen years older than she, bald, unattractive, and not at all her type. Here was an example of one of those "looks good on paper guys." This was going to be a LONG evening.

It was hard making small talk with him. He spilled his glass of wine. Her dinner arrived cold. Suddenly, they started laughing over the fact that everything was going wrong with the date. The laughter broke the ice, and they were able to enjoy the rest of the evening, plus she had great material with which to regale her friends the next day.

A good sense of humor is crucial in dealing with life's complexities, so try to find the funny. Humor is also a useful mechanism for binding people together. A little laughter goes a long way in reducing stress, even for a little while.

Exercise. Jane walked around the ellipse in Washington, D.C., on her lunch hour. Each day, she passed the same man who sat on a park bench reading. On her fourth circle around, they exchanged smiles, then words, and finally phone numbers. This was an added benefit to the ones we usually think about when discussing exercise.

We have jogged and walked our way through countless transitions in our lives, and it has helped us in numerous ways. We've grown physically stronger and psychologically calmer. Our weight is under control. If we started out stressed, we returned home more relaxed and better able to function. Both of us have done some of our best thinking while walking briskly. Take a brisk ten-to-fifteen-minute walk during your lunch hour, or whenever you can, and we'll guarantee you'll return feeling energized, more focused, and relaxed.

Relaxation. Some like Tai Chi to help them relax. Others swear by yoga. Still others enjoy meditating. Here's something that will lower your stress immediately: breathe in deeply six times, concentrating on inhaling and exhaling each to the count of six. As you inhale say, "I am cool (or warm if that's a better fit)" and as you exhale say, "I am calm." Doing this simple exercise whenever you feel the tension mounting will make you feel both calmer and more focused. Try it several times during the day.

Enough is enough. Are you drinking too much? Have your friends stopped calling? Are they all too busy to meet you for dinner? Are you constantly feeling sorry for yourself? Are people telling you that you've got to stop thinking about *him*? These are all telltale signs that you may be getting stuck in a depressed mode, berating and blaming yourself, obsessed with what you did wrong, and able to think about nothing but how miserable you are. You are also making your friends miserable. People can stand to hear the same story only so many times.

It may be time to get counseling to work through some of these feelings. Sometimes it's just too hard to break out of this stuck position by yourself. Ilene was in this position six months after her breakup with a man she thought she loved. She was unable to move forward and constantly complained about her wretched life. Her friends got sick of hearing it, and either stopped calling or found a quick reason to hang up as soon as the conversation turned to "woe is me."

Finally, she sought the assistance of a professional. Within a short time and input from her therapist, she decided to become a volunteer so she could stop focusing on herself and do something for someone else. Knowing she made someone's life a little better was a gratifying feeling.

Then it became a ripple effect. As soon as she started feeling better about herself, she was able to rejoin friends and activities. If you don't want to seek counseling, you can do what another friend did—pick up a stranger at a bar, just to remind yourself that you're still a good-looking babe!

Dos and Don'ts of Coping

Do

- Analyze what went wrong.
- Distract yourself with other activities.
- Look back with humor.
- Engage in positive self-talk.

Don't

- Rebound into another relationship right away.
- Blame yourself.
- Burden your friends too much with your angst.
- Resort to food or alcohol to ease the pain.

Chapter Five

Let's get Physical . . . If You Can

Eventually, if all goes well, and you meet someone you like and who likes you enough to go out together, by mutual consent, several times, you're going to arrive at that inevitable question: *Should you or shouldn't you?*

Two sets of issues come into play here. One may be your own personal issues.

- "I haven't slept with anyone other than my spouse, and he's been dead for five years!"
- "I've gotten thick around the middle, and my thighs are puckered!"
- "I'm wondering if I even remember how to kiss a man!"

The other set of issues revolves around how you feel about *him*. Because sex is more emotional for women than men, women can be turned off physically by men who exhibit unpleasant personality traits (i.e. talking incessantly about past relationships, asking nothing about you, wanting you to pay exactly half of the check, down to counting pennies, constantly looking at other women). At the same time, otherwise charming men can possess petty, unimportant physical traits that function as turnoffs (halitosis, body odor, a host of other nonspecific "smells," dandruff, nose hair, ear hair, back hair, no hair, and so on) . . . or just lack that certain chemistry you're looking for.

Stephanie: There's no denying it. You can enjoy someone's personality and intellect but just feel no physical attraction. Believe me, I know. I tried so hard to be attracted to Norman, Roy, and Larry, but it wasn't to be. On the other hand, if all else is good in the relationship and there's some attraction, (you don't hear bells and whistles when he kisses you, but you're not totally turned off either) you may want to take a chance and see what develops.

Some women find when they really respect a man and like everything else about him, sex gets better over time. Others have had to end their otherwise good relationships because they couldn't sleep with a man without first feeling a strong physical attraction.

What constitutes sex? For some it's intercourse. For others it's physical intimacy. Our friend, Joyce, said that when her boyfriend was unable to have intercourse because of a physical problem, she still felt valued because of his hugging, kissing, and touching her.

There are many, many books out there that instruct women about their sexual needs, but we advise caution about viewing these as the Holy Grail. Every woman is unique in her feelings about sexual satisfaction. There is no right or wrong way to think or feel. Rather you must get in touch with the sexual part of yourself and decide what it is you desire. Whether you enjoy having intercourse hourly, nightly, weekly, monthly, or rarely, there's nothing wrong with you, and books or talk shows that tell you what "normal" is haven't got a clue. We know of women who have never had an orgasm because they assume they can't, and they're okay with it. So go for what makes you happy.

And ask for what you need. It's not just about them! You need to factor in that not all or even most men are good lovers. Some are bad kissers;

some are clueless about arousing a woman. They just want to have sex and go to sleep. Here's where you need to do a little educating. Sure it's hard to show a man where your clitoris is, but well worth the embarrassment. You may have to be more graphic when describing what arouses you, but it's important that you do. Don't settle, ladies.

Sexual Concerns to Get Over

- **Your self-consciousness**

Relax a little. What you consider a body flaw might well turn out to be a male turn-on. And as in any other situation, humor helps.

Marge had been seeing Edward for a few months, and it was time to get intimate. She was a wreck, worrying about what he would think of her body. As they began kissing and touching each other, she whispered, "Do you do fat thighs?" He burst out laughing, which broke the tension and enabled them both to get on with things pleasurably.

- **Performance issues**

Lewis was constantly late for his dates with Shelley. Yet his sexual behavior was just the opposite—he always climaxed within thirty seconds! To make matters worse, he never offered to help Shelley reach a climax, just left her dangling in the wind. She couldn't ask him to satisfy her, and after a couple of months, she broke up with him. Why did she wait so long, you might ask? For one thing, she was hoping this was just a temporary thing. He told her he was taking medication that affected his performance. This can certainly be a problem. Medication can affect performance. Stress can also be a factor.

At least that's what Harvey told Ilene when he couldn't get it up. "I swear, it never happened before," he claimed. Then he told her how much stress he had because of work-related problems. For the three months they dated, he was able to climax four out of twelve times. This man had a problem but wasn't willing to discuss it. She worried that he wasn't attracted to her. He denied it but not vehemently. The last time they tried to make love and he couldn't, he broke up with her, telling her he wasn't really into sex. If it's a new relationship, you've got to cut him some slack. Men get nervous, too! If it keeps occurring, you've got to have a conversation. If hugging is enough for you, that would surely take the pressure off your partner, at least for a while. However, if you are a sexual person, as most people are, at least at the start of a relationship, and do care about this man, buy a vibrator. Talk about your feelings.

Viagra, by the way, is a wonderful enhancement to lovemaking. If it works, it can help him overcome performance issues and change your sex life. If he uses it daily, however, beware. It can make you pretty sore!

- **The myths**

The Jewish-women don't like sex myth: Wrong! Jewish women like sex as much as non-Jewish women. It all depends on how good their partners are!

The small-penis myth: You're in the midst of your first lovemaking session and you look down and think, "Is this all there is?" Well, the truth is guys with small penises can be very good lovers. It's what they do with it that counts!

- **Confusing sexual attraction with love**

Deep down Myra knew Dick had some quirky traits, but the sex was better than anything she had ever experienced. She couldn't get enough of him. Each time was better than the last. He was at least ten years younger than anyone she had ever gone with, which could account for his staying power. She blocked out the quirky behavior for a while but soon realized that "quirky" was being generous. In reality, his behavior was abnormal and, yes, scary at times.

Let's face it, some guys have exceptional staying power and are terrific lovers. It is easy to think this must be love when you are so turned on by the sexual attraction. Susan's marriage to Fred was pretty much sexless, other than the times it took to make two babies. When she divorced him and began dating Errol, he brought her to levels of pleasure she'd never before experienced. He literally swept her off her feet into a second marriage. It started out fine, but when the magic of life in the bedroom wore off, she started seeing faults she hadn't noticed before. Soon the sexual feelings diminished, and the marriage ended soon thereafter.

Even the most passionate affairs diminish in intensity after a while. It's at that point that you either realize how important all the other things you like/love about each other are, or you realize that sexual attraction was all there was.

- **The conquest game**

Andi: Ted started out so promising, taking me to sporting events and trendy hot spots. We really had fun, and things were progressing nicely. I liked him a lot. Finally, after two months, I decided to sleep with him; and to my astonishment, I didn't hear from him for the next month. When he finally called, he said casually, 'Hi, it's Ted. Remember me?' I was so blown away and insulted. This was my first glimpse into the dysfunctional single scene.

It's hard to believe, but some men, even at the age of fifty, pursue a woman, wine and dine her, have sex with her, and drop her . . . ready to move on to the next victim. This was true of Adam, a successful attorney.

His pattern was to bed as many women as possible until the word got out about him. Now, no one would date him, and he realized that his reputation was ruined. He became depressed and entered therapy. After months of work, he decided to make amends for his behavior by calling every woman he'd slept with and apologize.

Unfortunately, Adam's story, while extreme, isn't that uncommon. There are men, highly flawed men, we might add, who feel validated only when they convince a woman to sleep with them. After that, they lose interest because they got what they needed and feel pressured to move on to keep their egos intact. These men have low self-esteem, no matter how successful they are in life.

We wish we could give you warning signs, but, sadly, there really aren't any. It's hard to distinguish between the guys who are genuinely interested in developing a relationship and the guys who are in for the quick ego boost. Be leery, however, of men who push to sleep with you, especially early on in a dating relationship. It's best to err on the side of caution. There's no hurry. If someone is truly interested, he'll go along with your desire to wait.

Now, if you find yourself facing an "Adam," and as soon as you sleep with him, the calls stop coming, don't overanalyze and beat up on yourself. Chances are it's *his* problem, and "if only" you'd done all the things you wish you'd done instead, nothing would have turned out differently.

Safe Sex: More Important than Good Sex

One major problem with sleeping with a man is the safety issue. How do you know he's telling the truth when he swears he hasn't been with a woman in over six months? Further, when he admits to having been with a woman or two, how do you know whom *she's* slept with? And so on.

There can be no compromising when it comes to safe sex. Anyone who is sexually active is at risk for sexually transmitted diseases (STDs). A man can have an STD and not even know it because there aren't always symptoms. Condoms are a must! Andi insists on an AIDS test before she becomes intimate with a man. You must be tough here, even when passions rise in the heat of the moment and they swear they're clean.

Julia was dating a man she cared for a lot, but he told her he occasionally dated and slept with other women. She agreed to spend the night with him, but with the stipulation that there would be no intercourse. He really liked her and respected her wishes, and they had a cuddly evening together. Anything's possible when there's true feeling for each other.

Getting Through the First Time

Okay, after you've decided you're going to take the plunge, fears and all, how will you proceed? Naturally, you'll be showered, wearing that new sexy underwear; it's time to toss the ones with holes. It might be helpful to have a drink to loosen up a little. Set a romantic mood. A few candles glowing in a darkened room (wrinkles don't show up in the dark), and some soft background music will surely help you to relax.

Now for the important question: *Should you fake an orgasm?* We have talked to many single women about this and gotten about as many "yes" answers as "nos." The decision is really up to you. If your history has been to generally reach an orgasm, and you don't have an orgasm during this first outing with a new person (because of nervousness, perhaps), be honest.

If you never have orgasms, you must decide if you're going to fake it now and forever more or tell him that's not the important part for you. If you fake it, and he wasn't a particularly good lover, he'll think he's doing just fine. You can also say you occasionally experience an orgasm, but the actual lovemaking is more important. Or you can say you can only have an orgasm by using a vibrator, if it's true, and it has nothing to do with his lovemaking prowess; it's how you've always been.

Diminished Desire

It's not uncommon to start off a relationship being extremely physically attracted to a man, only to find your desire is losing its intensity as you get to know him better. Even the most passionate lovers tone down after a while.

Think through what is happening. Is your relationship remaining strong in other areas? Do you still enjoy spending time with him?

There's nothing like a great sex partner, but it's especially pleasurable when sex is combined with compatibility in other areas as well. The first thing you need to determine is what the plusses and minuses are in this relationship. Some women fool themselves into thinking everything is good because they hate the thought of starting over. Trust your instincts! If you really are compatible with him, think about what's causing the loss of passion, and what you can do to rekindle the spark. Often, it's the sameness of things; couples get comfortable and end up doing the same old, same old, be it touching, kissing, or position. Don't view sex as taking care of his needs because that negates the fact that you, too, have needs.

Be creative. Sure it may take some thought and effort, but it could have a big payoff.

Dos and Don'ts of Getting Physical

Do

- Make sure any sex you have is safe sex.
- Think romantic. How about a weekend getaway alone together?

- Be willing to talk about what turns you on.
- Be willing to experiment with new positions and new sexual activities (we're not talking about ménage à trois here, just a little variation on the theme).
- First, praise him for all of his efforts in trying to satisfy you. Then you can tell him how to do it better!
- Try to rekindle the spark if it goes out. Go dancing to get the romantic juices warmed up.

Don't

- Think his performance issues are because you don't excite him. Always look at the whole picture before you start thinking something's wrong with you.
- Make a big issue about his inability to perform. If you talk about it too much it becomes a psychological burden, and he will *never be able to do it*!
- Feel compelled to have intercourse with a man just because you are spending the night with him. There are other ways to exchange affection.
- Feel you need to sleep with a man if you're not ready. On the other hand, if you think you'll never be ready to sleep with him, it may be time to end the relationship.
- View sex as taking care of his needs.

Chapter Six

Breaking Up Is Hard to Do

He's verbally abusive.

He's physically abusive.

You don't love him or even like him.

You have no common interests.

He's always putting you down.

You can't stand being around him.

You realize he's cheating on you.

You argue all the time.

He's controlling.

There are many reasons to break up with a man. Those listed above are pretty compelling ones, factors that make breaking up a relatively easy decision.

Then there are the *deal breakers*—the issues you find are just too important to overlook, even when everything else between you is fine. It takes a while to uncover deal breakers because they usually emerge subtly. He's so funny and adorable when you first meet him, for example, that you ignore the fact that you're an ardent liberal and his politics are to the right of Attila the Hun. It takes a while for you to realize that while living with him seemed like an enchanting possibility, living with Rush Limbaugh piped in loud and clear in your living room is a nightmare.

Religious differences, too, seem minimal at first but can loom larger and larger over time.

Children can become major deal breakers—if you don't like his, his don't like you, yours don't like him, or he doesn't like yours. You need a compassionate partner by your side caring for and about your children, especially if they are young and living at home. If he is constantly finding fault with them, that could be a valid deal breaker.

If you find his children spoiled and annoying, you might ask yourself whether you want to have them around for the rest of your life.

If, on the other hand, your children complain about him, investigate before you act. Talk to them and ferret out what they really feel and whether the grievances are justified. Children often sense vulnerabilities in their parents—especially after divorce—and capitalize on them. Make sure their complaints are legitimate before you declare the situation a deal breaker.

Sometimes deal breakers can seem petty. Marlene recalls falling in love with a man who was extremely disciplined in all areas of his life except one. He smoked and would not consider stopping. Just a silly habit. Such a small thing. But it turned out to be a deal breaker. She couldn't stand living with the mess, the smell, the discomfort, the health hazard of secondhand smoke, and the strong possibility of sharing a life with this man that was not going to be a long and healthy one. In this case, love did not conquer all. Other addictions—alcohol, sex, drugs—can be similar deal breakers.

And then there are the abstract reasons that make breaking up a more difficult exercise.

You've been dating a really nice guy, but you realize he's not the one. You know you've got to end it, but you don't know how. You hate hurting people's feelings, and he's very sensitive. Worse, you think he's really fallen for you.

How do you go about breaking the news?

Deliver the News in Person

We recently read about a new business that tells customers' spouses or lovers that their partners are breaking up with them "in a direct, yet sympathetic manner, providing three reasons for the breakup and telling them their client wants no further contact with them." This agency charges $25 for news of the breakup by phone and $63 for news in person.

One woman we know told her boyfriend, "Farewell, it is over," in a short voice mail. Another chose e-mail as her venue for dumping. Yet another just didn't return his phone calls.

These "indirect" approaches might be justified for someone who has been mean or abusive or out there cheating on you, but only under such circumstances. For all those other men who don't make the grade, try to at least show a little respect and compassion. Breaking up is uncomfortable in a face-to-face situation, but it is kinder to do it that way.

It's also therapeutic. What you need here is closure, and the only way to get it is to either answer the questions he has about what went wrong or get answers from him to the questions you have. If you can't say the words, write a letter that states them clearly. Deliver it in person, and be there to talk about things when he finishes reading it.

Learn From the Experience

Andi: I met Kenneth on Jdate. He was sixteen years older than I, but I liked his profile. He seemed solid and mature. We had dinner at a trendy D.C. hotspot and drinks at a bar afterward. We instantly connected, and conversation flowed effortlessly and easily. We had a strong attraction to each other. In the following eight weeks, we spent a lot of time together, at parties, on his boat, out with friends, and having quiet dinners. He introduced me to his kids. He called twice a day. He was open about expressing his feelings for me and told me how deeply connected he felt to me. But then, things started changing. When I noticed the change, he admitted that my three young kids were an issue. His youngest was thirteen, and he said when the boy turned eighteen, he wanted the freedom to do what he wanted and not be held back. He felt he had already paid his dues and raised two kids, and he was done. I was surprised after he had told me so many times that he felt so connected to me and had never felt so close to a woman before. I didn't understand the fast dating pace and the serious talks when he wasn't interested in my whole package with my kids.

Breaking up with Kenneth was a painful experience, but a learning experience. I learned that when something seems too good to be true, it just might be.

I learned that when you are faced with a huge disappointment, it is good to give yourself time to grieve before heading back to the dating scene.

I realized dating is about taking chances, and there is always the risk of getting hurt. I had gotten swept away in the moment of wonderful weekends, great chemistry, and believing all the flattering things he said. It is hard to stay grounded when everything feels so right. I asked myself how I would handle things next time. I decided I would hold back a little and not give 100 percent of myself so quickly. If possible, I would do it in stages.

Sarah Jane had grown increasingly annoyed with Artie, her boyfriend of sixteen months. She just didn't have the heart to break up with him. He was driving her crazy with his annoying habits and controlling behavior. Her friends couldn't stand him. Her children couldn't stand him. Even *his* children couldn't stand him! Still, she felt, he was annoying but not evil; and she worried that if she broke up with him, he'd have no one.

"What are we doing this weekend?" he asked her one night after a heated discussion.

"WE are doing nothing," she said in an exasperated tone. "I need some time to myself."

That was the beginning, a show of anger and a rejection, but only for the weekend. It gave Artie time to mull things over, time to see the handwriting on the wall, to brace himself for what might be coming.

The next weekend, Sara Jane told him things weren't working out, and she wanted more time to sort things out. After that, she stayed on message and suggested he get on with his life.

Ease His Fall

There are ways to break up and still leave a man's self-esteem intact. Choose the right words—honest ones, but kind ones. "I've enjoyed getting to know you, and think you are a really nice man, but I don't see us together for the long term." If he questions you as to why, you might be abstract. "I guess there's something missing for me, and I just have to trust my instincts."

Let's Be Friends?

Whether or not you can remain friends depends on the kind of relationship you had. If there were a lot of passion and the breakup is causing one of you a great deal of pain, it is better to break things off entirely and go your separate ways. If you had a lot in common, just not a lot of passion for each other, then friendship is a definite possibility and a way of easing him away slowly.

If he's a nice guy but just not *your kind* of guy, you might try fixing him up with your single friends. That can be a very kind way to break up because it lets him know that he is valued. And who knows? It could turn out to be a match.

Don't Procrastinate

Connie told us that as she gets older and life gets shorter, she is learning to be more direct. She used to remain in relationships because she didn't know how to break them off in a way that wasn't hurtful. Now she's learned not to waste any time in a bad relationship.

Connie has a point. When it is over, it's over. Delaying the bad news does nothing for you and nothing for your partner either. Be firm and honest. The best way to get over what could be a traumatic situation—either his or yours—is to be decisive and move on quickly.

Sometimes procrastination leads to bad behavior. Michelle was starting to really care for Ron. He was a wonderful companion, treated her like a queen, called her frequently, and seemed to care for her a lot. Things were progressing nicely when suddenly he stopped calling.

When Michelle called him, instead of telling her he had lost interest, he told her he had just been too busy working and hadn't had time to socialize. Believing him, Michelle made the mistake of inviting him to dinner with some of her friends. He showed up late, complained nonstop about his ex-wife, told everyone he would never again trust a woman, and made a negative comment when Michelle ordered a second glass of wine. Then he wolfed down his dinner and berated her for allowing him to eat so much when she knew he was supposed to be on a diet.

Wouldn't it have been more pleasant if he had just told Michelle once his interest had begun to wane that he wanted to break things off?

Charlotte just couldn't find the words to tell Mel it was over. She tried at several different times during the evening but simply could not come up with the right words to do so. Finally, when he took his overnight bag out of the trunk, she burst out, "Don't bother bringing that bag out! You won't be needing it anymore!"

(Hardly the most tactful way to tell a man the relationship was over.)

Andi: I'd been dating Donald for a few months and knew he just wasn't for me. I was in an airport line, obsessing to my friend via cell phone about the best way to tell him. Suddenly, four strangers, also standing in line chirped up, "Call him now; get it over with; you'll feel so much better." So I did and got his voice mail. "Leave a message," they told me, and I did. I told him how much I valued him as a friend, and that I enjoyed his company, but I wasn't in love with him. As soon as I hung up, the strangers were high-fiving me; it was quite a scene. I felt like I was in a sitcom! The next day I called him, and we talked for quite a while. He said he understood my feelings. Certainly, being honest helped, and we hoped to remain friends.

Are You SURE You Want to Break Up?

First and second and even third impressions can be misleading. Before you take steps to end a relationship, ask yourself whether you might be getting a little impatient. Are you too ready to "move on"? Have you given this man enough of a chance? Many differences can be accommodated over time. Many superficial complaints seem inconsequential when a relationship grows in more significant ways. You don't want to let a good one get away because of an unwillingness to take the time to really get to know him.

If you find you are dating a lot but constantly rejecting guys because of little flaws, it may be time for some introspection. Are you shying away from commitment? Have you mentally carved out an image of Mr. Perfect that is a little too perfect for a human being live up to? Do you really want to meet someone? Are you protecting yourself from being hurt? This is a good time to find out what YOUR issues are. If you can't do it alone, get a therapist to help. It could be the best money you ever spent!

There is no easy way to tell a man that the relationship is over. No matter how gently you try to put it, his feelings will be hurt. But once you have made the decision, it's better to be up front about it.

Dos and Don'ts of Breaking Up

Do

- Be truthful, but offer honesty with a dash of kindness.
- Tell him in person, if possible.
- Take responsibility for your share of causing this breakup.
- Answer his questions and ask yours. Make this a learning experience.
- Analyze what happened. Is this part of a dating pattern?
- Be open to change, but don't change your values.
- Try to leave the relationship remembering the good times.
- Move on, avoiding the mistakes made in the past.

Don't

- Pick a fight just to have an excuse to break up.
- Have someone else tell him.
- Say, "It's not you, it's me!"
- Try to get even.
- Do it in a public place.
- Keep tabs on him after the breakup.
- Try to hold on if your partner wants to end the relationship.
- Delay telling him it's over once you're sure.
- Try to "be friends" after an intense romance.
- Bad-mouth him to others. Move on.
- Rebound into another relationship right away.

Chapter Seven

Resources for Meeting Men

- You're ready to get out there and date, but don't know where to begin.
- You've heard about online dating but wonder how safe it is.
- You've asked all your friends but no one knows any single men.

What should you do?

There's no limit, these days, to the places you can meet men if you are open to the idea that connections can be made anywhere. You might strike up a conversation at a dinner party with a couple who decide you would be the perfect match for their cousin. Your child's third grade teacher might think you'd be just right for her brother. You just might meet one at the gym if you're on the look out. (Your time on the elliptical will go much faster if you strike up a conversation with the man working out next to you!) You could meet guys at funerals—although we advise against flirting with the one who is mourning his newly departed wife. Shop for a man at the supermarket! The good looking one who is buying a single lamb chop or several frozen "dinners for one" might be a good prospect.

Andi: "*Some single women have a hard time finding a date while others have no problem meeting men. What makes the difference? For one thing, it's who you know and who they know—your social network is very important. Fix—ups are always good because you generally get some information about the prospective guy. I have been fixed up 50 plus times within the past few years and I have met several interesting people who have filled this book! It is a great way to meet people. Some of my most outrageous dates were fix-ups, and I learned that sometimes the matchmakers don't know these men well at all. When you hear, "I have a great guy for you," don't get your hopes up. Great is usually in the eye of the beholder. Yet, I always agree to be fixed up because you never know and it only takes one! Besides, when someone can vouch for the person you are being setting up with, it gives him a little more credibility.*"

Here are some other conventional resources that have worked for women we know.

- **Singles hiking, biking, bird-watching or sailing groups**: If you like the outdoors, physical activity and communing with nature, most communities have groups organized who take part in outdoor activities like these. The good news is they are good ways to find men who like to do what you like to do . . . IF you like to do it. And that "if" is a big one. Don't sign up for a bicycle outing if you don't like riding a bicycle, for example, or sign on to a sailing trip if you get seasick!
- **Museum courses for singles**: Many museums offer courses for single people. They're generally well presented and well attended. The trick is to go more than once so that you begin seeing familiar faces.
- **Parents Without Partners**: This is a large national organization with affiliates in communities across the nation. It's a good way to meet someone who is also a parent and therefore has similar

concerns and interests. The downside is that more women than men usually show up for meetings and group activities.

- **Singles dances:** The key here is to go with a smile on your face, a song in your step and body language that says you're outgoing, fun to be with, available and absolutely *love* to dance. Do not stand awkwardly on the sidelines!

- **Singles nights at bars:** This is not something you want to do alone, but with a girlfriend who is also interested in meeting men to keep you company just in case no one looks interesting or interested. This could be a perfectly enjoyable way to spend an evening.

- **Dining at a bar**. This is different than sitting at a bar with a drink in your hand waiting for someone to talk to you. Lots of people who are alone or don't have a reservation for the dining room will eat at the bar. You're there for dinner and it's a great way to connect with someone who happens to find himself sitting next to you. Be sure to smile and show open body posture.

- **Volunteer**. Do you care about the environment? Cleaning up the park near your house? Tutoring children who need help? Raising money for a charity important to you? The fact is, any activity that gets you out and into a public place augments your chances of meeting someone, so by all means if there is a community issue that interests you, get involved! You just might find yourself accomplishing two goals by actively pursuing one.

- **Place a personal ad**. Most local newspapers and magazines have pages reserved for personal ads in which you can specify what you are like and the type of person you are looking for. When placing one, be sure you can screen responses through the magazine—in other words, without giving out your address or phone number. Try to meet respondents who sound interesting during daylight hours and at a public place—a restaurant, bar, or coffee house.

- **Get a dating coach**. Charging rates similar to professional counselors ($75—$150 an hour) dating coaches work with clients on ways to meet and attract long-term partners. The theory is, just as you'd hire a piano teacher if you want to learn to play the piano, so you should hire a dating coach if you feel you need help developing the kinds of body language, communication skills, confidence, and street smarts you need to attract the man of your dreams.

- **Hire a match-maker**. For centuries, "match-makers" have helped arrange suitable marriages between single people in nearly every culture around the world. Today's modern match-makers are often local services who, for a fee, will interview both men and women extensively and then look through their many resumes and try to set members up with the "perfect person."

- **Sign on for a pricey dating service.** Not worth it! There are so many other resources out there and more expensive is not really any better! What is more, dating services tend to have a limited supply of eligible people, so despite all the time they take "getting to know you," they often can't come up with someone your type. One woman we know signed up with a dating service that guaranteed 20 dates a year for $1,500. She filled out forms indicating the type of man she was looking for. She was a respected economist. So who was she fixed up with? A produce salesman! Not that there's anything wrong with produce salesmen, but it was like mixing apples and oranges—or should we say tomatoes and statistics?

The Internet

Nothing has had a bigger impact on the way men and women meet than the Internet. The idea behind the many dating websites is to unite—through self-choice—that huge pool of men out there looking for women with that huge pool of women out there looking for men. Sometimes it happens. Sometimes it doesn't. Since there is, after all, no guarantee that Mr. Right is who he says he is, Internet dating requires abundant hope tinged with a healthy layer of skepticism, persistence, time, a shrewdly composed self profile, and an eternally positive outlook that HE is out there, and if you are just patient enough, you will eventually find him. It's also a way to meet a lot of not-perfect-but-still-entertaining men along the way.

But the world of the Internet is a vast one, populated by who-knows-what, and therefore precautions should be taken:

1) *Post a picture that is attractive but really looks like you, and be honest in describing yourself and your interests when you write your personal ad.* You are not creating an advertisement designed to attract the most replies possible, after all; you are hoping to attract men who will be drawn to your true personality and share your interests. Neither exaggerate nor under-rate. Describe your personality traits, whether you are outgoing and friendly, or more reserved and introverted. Include activities and hobbies you enjoy doing. Omit sexual terms like passionate, sensual, sexy. These send a message you may not intend and will attract men you may not be looking for. How honest you should be? You don't need to write that you have Herpes in the ad, unless you're writing for a Herpes Singles Group. Some things are better left unsaid . . . at first.

2) *Get a free e-mail account just for dating responses.* If you want to go beyond communicating on the dating website, then provide an e-mail address that is not your regular one—sign on to gmail, Hotmail, or Yahoo—and don't use your full name. This will protect your privacy and also stop your regular mailbox from overflowing.

3) *Only use paid online services.* There are a lot of Internet dating services now that are free, but since men who sign on don't even

need to identify themselves with a credit card, there is no way to screen participants, and an open invitation, therefore, for some non-savory types to sign on.

4) *Be on the alert for married men*. The most common clues lie in their reticence to disclose things about themselves. Married men won't post a picture, for example, for fear of being spotted by someone who knows them. They won't reveal a last name. They will be abstract about where they live, where they work.

5) *In the initial stages of communications, guard your identity*. A little information can be used to uncover a lot of information—your income, the value of your home, where you work, and so on. There is no harm in taking extra precautions before you get to really know someone.

6) *Evaluate*. What kind of personality is he evidencing in his e-mail? Does he have a sense of humor? Does he seem abrupt? Easy to anger? Did he lie in any way about his profile? Pay close attention and trust your gut instincts.

7) *Take it with a grain of salt*. A lot of Internet profiles are similar in what they say. Many will tell you they are looking for "someone honest, loyal, attractive, and independent, to be a best friend, possibly leading to a long-term relationship." Keep in mind that everyone tries to put his best foot forward and that probably means misrepresenting himself. Many use touched up pictures. A good rule of thumb is that some may actually look like the pictures they post, but no one will look better than the picture he posts!

8) *Meet in a public place*. If everything about him seems positive and you have progressed from e-mail to telephone conversations to actually deciding the time has come to meet, do so in a bar, restaurant, or coffee house, tell a friend where you will be, and arrange to get there on your own. Never let him pick you up at home on the first date.

Andi: *"What's fun about dating on the Internet is coming home every night and finding interesting e-mail from prospective dates. It's sort of like dating in the comfort of your home. After a while I learned how to go through and pick men who seemed to be my type. I also learned to be leery of certain pictures. Some men put pictures of themselves that were taken about 10 years ago! Of course I couldn't know this until meeting them for the first (and last) time. Someone seems to have told Internet daters that women are attracted to men who are good with children, because many men post pictures of themselves with children. I discovered that that often these were not only men who had no children, but men who confessed to me later when they found out I had 3 children, that they weren't interested in anyone with children. They had just wanted to make a good impression by appearing with their nieces or nephews!"*

There are many, many Internet dating sites—sites for just about every ethnic and religious background. (Just put "Internet Dating Sites" into your computer search engine and you will find them.) Here are a few of the most common ones:

eHarmony.com

This website was among the first to use a "compatibility matching system." Potential members complete a highly detailed questionnaire, which is supposed to help you find your perfectly compatible partner, and the website then suggests matches for you. More spiritual than other sites, and more for people seeking partners than people seeking fun dates, eHarmony boasts that a high percentage of its members go on to "happily ever after" marriages.

LavaLife.com

On this user friendly site, which is geared more toward sex, you can sign up for three different areas: Dating, Relationships, or Intimate Encounters.

Members can post their profile in any of the three, or in all of the three. Each area is displayed separately in the main menu, making navigation very easy. Members do the "matching" themselves here, responding to the profiles that attract them.

JDate.com

This popular Jewish dating service contains thousands of profiles which are separated according to region. Profiles include details on age, relationship status, education, occupation, and answers to more abstract questions, with search and matching features that enable you to meet people your age and in your area.

Match.com

This well known online dating site, endorsed by Dr. Phil, has a large active user base and focuses on relationships as well as dating—both friendships and romances. It offers surveys designed to match up couples and searching abilities, where members describe themselves in a select number of key words and use the online search engine to find those qualities in others.

PerfectMatch.com

The easy to navigate site's patented Duet Total Compatibility System helps match prospective daters based on personality traits, lifestyle values, love goals, and a plethora of other important things. Relationship expert Dr. Pepper Schwartz is *PerfectMatch.com*'s leading spokesperson, advocating that their services are "the intelligent way to approach online dating."

Prime Singles. net

Silversingles.com

These are website for older daters—50-plus years. You can send messages anonymously, post your profile on a message board, and engage in over-50 chat rooms. The site also does two way matching.

Big Church.com

This site for Christian singles boasts more than half a million members worldwide and encourages participants to search for those who share their spiritual beliefs.

SciConnect.com

This single network is geared to science professionals as well as people who are interested in science and nature. "The world is a crowded Petri dish," the website announces, "and yet for those of an intellectual bent who happen to be single, it's not easy, especially past university age, to find *that certain microbe* for a great symbiotic relationship." Age range is 20-80.

Prepare

When you buy a house or a car or a major appliance, you do your research, studying ads and comparing possibilities. You look at what's out there and at what price and with what types of guarantees.

Before signing up for online dating, it's important to do similar research. Go to your computer. Visit many sites and compare.

Analyze the men and their profiles. Do these men sound like ones you might be interested in? What do they choose to tell about themselves? What kinds of women are they looking for? Are there recurrent themes in the profiles? Do any of the men appeal to you? (Don't be surprised if you see some you know!)

Analyze the women's profiles. What do they choose to reveal about themselves? Do these seem like your type? Which profiles do you like, and which ones would you skip if you were a man? (Feel free to plagiarize some of their ideas if you like. After all, you're going to have to write a profile too.)

Post a profile

Your profile is your online resume. This is a marketing tool designed to enable you to find the man you want. You don't want to lie, but you do want to accentuate the positive. Make a list of the good qualities about yourself and be savvy about it, with an eye toward those qualities that might appeal to someone else. Think about your goals and values. Think of some of the characteristics your friends compliment you about. Focus also on your audience.

Then think of ways to make your profile interesting. You want to stand out, after all. Check other profiles for ideas. Profile-writing is often easier (and more fun) to do if you do it with the help of a friend or two.

Next you'll need a picture. Here again, you don't want to lie, but you do want to accentuate the positive. You want to look good, but you want to look like yourself. You want him to be able to *recognize you* when you meet him for a date!

Read Between the Lines

- If they respond "probably not" to the question asking if they want children, it means definitely not.
- If they are looking for women who are 10 plus years younger and won't consider women their own age, they are probably looking for arm candy to help their aging egos.
- If they say that loyalty and honesty are the most important qualities, it may mean their former mate cheated on them.
- If they're mainly interested in fun and excitement, they probably aren't ready for a real relationship.
- If they say they're in their "late" 40s, 50s or 60s, it most likely means they're older.
- If he writes, as one man did, that he was looking for a "sexy, energetic, beautiful lady with thick hair, who's athletic and a good cook and will make me laugh," run the other way. You will never satisfy a man so demanding of perfection.
- The personality section is very telling as well. If someone admits that he tends to be a bit argumentative (which people do), count it as another red flag. This man may be honest, but he also may be trouble!
- In the free time section, if he says he loves gambling, poker, Vegas, ask yourself if you're in the mood for a risk-taker. If he says he's a rock climber, before you get carried away with the image of a handsome, athletic outdoorsman, ask yourself if you are going to want to join him. In other words, look for someone who loves to do the things you love to do. Someone who enjoys lazy Sunday mornings might be a couch potato, but at the same time, he might be more your type!
- The section asking about their reading preferences can also be revealing.

Additionally, you may want to check out a couple of books:

- "Finding Your Perfect Match", by Pepper Schwartz whose website was mentioned above.
- "Flings, Frolics and Forever After: A Single Woman's Guide to Romance After Fifty", by Katherine Chaddock.
- "Love Smart" by Dr. Phil McGraw

Pros and cons of Internet Dating

Pros

- It's fun to come home each night and be greeted by a whole bunch of electronic prospects.
- There's a large pool of available men.
- You've got some control about whom you'll see and whom you won't.
- It's very entertaining to shop for men in your pjs.

Cons

- It's exhausting to come home each night and be greeted by a whole bunch of electronic prospects.
- There's a large pool of nerds.
- The person you decide to see may be a bad choice!
- Sometimes it's hard to differentiate between the good guys and the bad ones, because they all write about themselves in glowing terms. This can result in a bad date that's a waste of your time. Then you may need to do some reframing (see chapter 4).

Dina, a woman in her late fifties who has never been married, refuses to do online dating. She feels more comfortable meeting someone in "her world", small though it is. So Dina relies on meeting people through friends because at least they'd have something in common—the friends. The problem with this approach is that greatly limits the possibilities. Dina hasn't gone out in a while. We hope that Dina will take a risk and expand her network by trying online dating.

Lenore used a dating service in which a match was made with a guy she had dated 10 years before! They ended up dating for a year, but in time, she remembered why it didn't work the first time around.

Dos and Don'ts

Do

- Check the dating pool of the website before signing on to be sure it's large and includes many in your area.
- Read his on-line ad very carefully.

Don't

- Pretend to be something you're not. If you aren't intellectual and don't like opera, don't say you do (even if you've always *wanted* to). You will meet someone you have nothing in common with.
- Respond to someone who loves long walks on the beach if you are allergic to sand.
- Be discouraged by meeting men who are not what they say they are or not what you want them to be. Stick with it. Many lasting relationships have started on the Internet!

Chapter Eight

Aging Dating

- You've been married to the same man for forty years, and he died.
- You're a new divorcee, just turned fifty, and you want to get back out there but are scared to death.
- You haven't been intimate with anyone other than your spouse, and the thought of being with someone new freaks you out.
- Someone fixed you up on what will be your first date in thirty-five years, and you're nervous, sweating profusely, and trying to think of something to talk about.

Well, join the club. You are most certainly not alone. There are more than 35 million Americans over the age of fifty out there who are single, many of whom are probably going through the same jitters you are.

What's more, the fact that you're *not* a nubile young twenty-something anymore is actually good news. Oh sure, your skin might not look as smooth and taut and resilient as it did back then, but on the inside you are in much better shape, much better prepared to take on this dating thing.

You are emotionally more intelligent, for starters. Experience has made you a more able socializer, a more comfortable conversationalist. You aren't overrun by those hormones anymore, which were the cause of so many bad youthful decisions. You are clued into life's realities.

And you know what? So is he. There are some glaring exceptions to the rule out there, of course, but for the most part, single men fifty and over are less impulsive, more pensive, patient, and compassionate than their younger selves and are dating because they yearn for companionship more than for any other reason. What is more, studies show mature men are much shyer in general than they were in their youth.

So, instead of fretting, let's just get out there and check out the situation.

Nikki was a young widow at sixty. She started walking to help her deal with her grieving. She passed a man walking in the opposite direction. Since they lived in the same neighborhood, she passed him day after day. They started talking. He was a tall, good-looking seventy-five-year-old who had recently been widowed. They began walking together. Amazing what you might meet on your own neighborhood sidewalk if you just pay attention!

Women who become single at midlife, whether by design or surprise, need to forge a new identity and rebuild their lives. Some rediscover their sexuality after having spent many years in a dead marriage. Some thrive on their newly acquired independence. Some date in hopes of finding a romantic relationship, while others are just looking for occasional male companionship.

What will you do with the many productive years ahead of you? When you make a choice, you put yourself in charge, and there's nothing like being in control of your life. They say there are three types of people—those who make it happen, those who watch it happen, and those who say, "What happened?" If you want to meet a man and don't have a social network that can introduce you to available men, you've got to get out there with a smile on your face and a glimmer in your eye.

You will need

- To replace your fear of rejection with a "who cares?" attitude—Who cares if this one isn't interested? There are plenty more out there!
- To be more aggressive about making connections and upbeat and positive when meeting the opposite sex.
- To take greater care of your appearance. Buy some new clothes. Get your hair done. Get in shape. This is not necessarily to attract a man (although, to be sure, it won't hurt) but rather to help you develop an enhanced sense of self—a fresh beginning.
- To be strategic—figuring out "where the men are" and going there, be it a book club, a bridge club, an adult class, golf or tennis lessons, a political rally, or an Internet dating site.

That Window of Opportunity

Like you, most men in this age group have not been single forever. Most are widowers or divorcees, and that raises an issue that was not part of your youthful dating past: How much time should elapse between the time his wife left him—or he left her—in a bitter divorce and the time when he should be ready to start dating again? No one wants to walk into a hornet's nest. Absorbing the anger intended for the former wife does not make for a pleasant dating experience or bode well for a future together. Nor does hearing about what happened, over and over again.

In the same way, how much time should elapse between the time his wife dies and the time when the widower is ready to meet someone special? Many who have gone after newly widowed men say the funeral is too soon, but waiting until the luncheon following the funeral is too late. Should you join the "casserole brigade," the women who visit new widowers bearing meals? We've known cases where this has worked, but there are lots of variables, such as, did you know the man before his wife died? Walk into a stranger's house bearing brisket, and you will be looked at suspiciously.

Many widowers aren't ready to date for a long time, even though they think they are. Our friend, Emma, was fixed up with a widower whose wife had died six months earlier. "He was a maudlin mess," she complained, "clearly still in the throes of grief, consumed with love for his departed wife, the 'angel,' and not in any mood to meet another woman."

Emma thanked the person who fixed her up and told her friend that while she found him attractive and interesting, she thought it best not to see him again until he had moved on somewhat. "Let's talk again in six months," Emma suggested.

Her timing was slightly off. Three months later, he was introduced to a different woman; and six months after Emma's date with him, he and the other woman were in a serious relationship.

Emma's experience underscores the fact that navigating the "window of opportunity" between when a man breaks up with or loses his wife and when he's ready to enter into a new relationship is an inexact science at best!

Age-Related Issues

We may be more confident about the knowledge we have acquired over the years—shrewder about human nature, more certain about our likes and dislikes than we were when we were young—but we are probably a good deal *more self-conscious about our bodies* than we were when we were young, especially if we haven't revealed them to anyone but one man for a long time. The body that provoked awed stares in a bikini, way back when, you might very well prefer to reveal these days in long sleeves and slacks.

Remember, though, that he, too, is carrying around a "more mature" version of his former body. Joking about things might help break the ice. "How about a blindfold to help your tactile sense become sharper?" sixty-seven-year-old Anne asked her new boyfriend when they were about to become intimate.

He found that very funny . . . and kind of comforting.

If you are entering the dating scene after many years of being married to the same person, and you're old enough to think of a condom as strictly a birth control method, you might be feeling very *self-conscious about having the safe sex conversation*—at least the first time you have it. It is normal to feel self-conscious, but essential to have the conversation before being intimate with anyone. How many sexual partners has he had? If he has been sexually active, when was his most recent AIDS test? Did he bring a condom with him? If you are uncomfortable asking such questions, think of how much more self-conscious you would feel with a sexually transmitted disease!

Older women need to be prepared for sexual aberrations (as do younger women). Wendy was set up with Ben by a mutual friend. He had a sterling reputation, and all the fine qualities one would seek in a mate. The first date went fine. On the second date, he came in and asked to put something in her refrigerator. After they had gone out, he came back to her home and told her he wanted to change into something more comfortable while she made coffee. She was somewhat perplexed but consented. He reappeared with shorts on. Then he told her that he had some special medication in the fridge that he used to pump up his penis. Wendy, who wasn't too savvy in the dating world, was shocked and clearly not ready for a sexual relationship on a second date, let alone with someone with a pumped-up penis! Needless to say, no coffee was served.

While sexual enhancement products (Viagra, Cialis, pumps, and what have you) have enriched the sex lives of both men and women, some dating etiquette is in order. Granted, these products have given men a new lease on life and maybe they want to make up for what they've missed, but timing is important!

Health is also an age-related dating issue. "In sickness and in health, 'til death do us part" is an easier vow to take when you are young. Commitment at a later age, when long-term health is an iffy proposition, requires some forethought.

Sophie met Al when he was sixty-eight, surely young by today's standards. The first three years were idyllic; they traveled, went out to dinner and the theatre regularly, and had a host of friends. Then Al developed Alzheimer's disease. Life changed drastically. Most of their friends no longer wanted to go out with them; going to dinner was often embarrassing as Al frequently forgot his table manners, travel was too difficult, and Sophie became a lonely and frazzled caregiver.

While many older men retain their vitality and sexual desire into their nineties, generally, the sex appeal of the "older man" may decrease with age. They may have seemed more sophisticated, with higher earnings and more developed careers than younger men when we were young, but in late-life dating, the older the man, the more likely he is to get sick and require attention during the later stages of life. Many women looking forward to wonderful "new beginnings" when they marry older men the second time around find their lives drastically curtailed when they are forced to become their new husbands' caregivers.

Friends tend to advise women who are dating older men to refrain from marrying them, just in case. Some women take the advice, and some don't.

Harriet's friends were concerned when she married an eighty-one-year-old man. Sure, he was in great shape—biking, swimming, and working out regularly—but at eighty-one, anything could happen. But Harriet was in love and waved away her friends' concerns.

Shortly after their marriage, Harriet's back gave out, and she had major back surgery. As soon as she recovered from that, she developed tremendous pain in her leg and now required hip-replacement surgery. Guess who became the caregiver?

There are no clear answers as to the right path to follow. We know many couples enjoying life to the fullest in their eighties and nineties! What's important is to make a decision based on facts as well as feelings. Try to imagine how you'll feel if you're no longer able to enjoy things as a couple. Will you be able to handle it?

Adult children swear they want their single parent to be happy, but happy on whose terms? Happy with whom and under what conditions? When "happiness" becomes more specific, many adult children interfere—sometimes to protect their mother and sometimes to protect what they see as their inheritance.

Ruth Ann, a widow, met Frank, a divorcee, at a bridge lesson. She had been single for seven years and anxious to meet someone. She and Frank had so much in common; they both had three grown children, grandchildren, and shared an enjoyment of bridge and golf. Frank was a man of modest means and lived simply. Ruth Ann had inherited a lot of money from her late husband. They started seeing each other, and things were going so well until Ruth Ann told her children about Frank. She was shocked when they not only weren't happy for her but dissuaded her from continuing the relationship. What Ruth Ann finally discovered was that her children were fearful of losing their inheritance.

Adult children may also interfere because they feel roles have been reversed, that in a sense they are your guardian. Be careful what you tell them. If you have some concerns about the man you're seeing, you can bet they will have more. If you resolve those concerns, then they won't let you forget them. Better not to let your adult children become confidantes. You just might shock them!

Sally and Manny really hit it off and began seeing each other regularly. When he asked her to go away with him for the weekend, she called her daughter to help her buy a new nightgown. (It had been about twenty-five years since she last purchased one.) Her daughter picked out a number of conservative peignoir sets, but Sally wasn't interested. Her daughter picked out some silky pajamas, but again, Sally said, "No, no, that's not what I want."

"What DO you want?" asked her daughter, exasperated by now.

"Oh, I see what I want," Sally said, and while her daughter stared in disbelief, Sally grabbed a clingy, very short nightie with shoestring straps.

So Many Possibilities!

Young couples are expected to get engaged. Engaged couples are expected to get married. Married couples are expected to make children, raise them, and live happily ever after. The beauty of "older" dating is there is no pattern you have to follow, no rituals you have to observe. You can carve out whatever relationship works for you. Are you looking for a wild sexual fling?

Just do it.

Carol was married to Sheldon, a successful albeit self-centered businessman, for twenty-five years. She was the dutiful wife, adroitly handling all the social occasions, raising the children, making sure Sheldon's in-town and in-the-country homes were beautifully cared for and ready for entertaining. When she was fifty, Sheldon announced that he was in love with the twenty-five-year-old investment analyst he'd hired. Carol was devastated. She felt old, used, over the hill, and put out to pasture. At her children's suggestion, she enrolled in a gym. A personal trainer took an interest in her, and she took an interest in him. They had a relatively short but extremely therapeutic affair that ended in a solid friendship. Today,

Carol feels younger than she has in years, pleased that she is no longer married to Sheldon, and looking forward to the future.

Many women who have lived in committed relationships for a long time miss the "commitment" but want a little freedom.

Kathy met Michael a few years after her husband, John, had died—enough years to miss the companionship of a spouse but enjoy the independence of a single person. She loved having someone who understood her, someone to compare notes with on books and politics and theater, someone to go out with, someone to be intimate with, but she never wanted to get married again. Fortunately, neither did Michael. They both enjoyed having their separate homes and their joint relationship.

Are you looking for the love of your life? That's a possibility too, even if you are at an age most would consider "over the hill."

Ed was a seventy-nine-year-old widower, Gert a seventy-five-year-old widow. Both had spent more than fifty years in very strong marriages. Both were devastated by their spouses' deaths. Both were also young for their ages, vibrant, and good looking. What they shared was a sense of bereavement, a sense of humor, and very similar pasts—long-term monogamous relationships, parental concerns about their children (who were the same ages) and grandchildren (who were the same ages). Both had been besieged by the opposite sex since the death of their spouses and were very uncomfortable about the prospect of "dating." They were introduced by Ed's wife's cousin. "You're miserable, she's miserable," he said. "Try being miserable together!"

What happened was anything but miserable. They may have been old hands at marriage, but they were new to each other. They had great sex, great love, abundant laughter, shared family occasions, and travels around the country and the world. Their children think the years they shared with each other may have been the best years of their lives.

Dos and Don'ts of Aging Dating

Do

- Carpe diem—seize the day. Approach new people at social gatherings. Be proactive and approachable.
- Dress for success, not failure. First impressions are important.
- Listen and ask questions. You will gain information and also appreciation (Men love to be asked about themselves.)
- Go into the fray with a game plan. Analyze your wish list. Itemize your "must haves" and your "can't stands" in terms of personality traits in a prospective suitor.
- Reject rejection. It happens to everyone. Taking it seriously wastes precious time.
- Be open to this new time. Be willing to try out new activities until you find what really excites you.

Don't

- Feel sorry for yourself for more than an hour at a time.
- Jump into something too quickly.
- Give up immediately if something is not right. Give it time.
- Tell anyone you're "looking for a serious relationship" on the first date!
- Just sit there if he spends the entire night talking about himself (Challenge him instead!).
- Have the maitre d' show you to five tables before you find one you like, i.e., don't be "high maintenance."
- Complain about past relationships.
- Extol past relationships.

Chapter Nine

What You See and Hear Isn't Always What You'll Get

Ah, romance. Falling in love is a wonderful feeling but unfortunately one that all too often inhibits the brain's receptors from taking in and analyzing important information.

Greta's politics have always been liberal verging on radical. Tim confessed right up front that he was very conservative. His kids are making millions running hedge funds. Greta's kids are saving the world for low to moderate incomes. They laughed over the difference.

Tim even (he admitted, rolling his eyes sheepishly) liked to listen to Rush Limbaugh from time to time.

They really got a chuckle over that one! After all, Tim was thoughtful, good looking, kind, caring, witty, and sexy too.

Isn't this hysterical, Greta thought to herself, *ME falling for a Rush Limbaugh fan!* "Oh, what does it matter?" she murmured, gazing up into Tim's light blue eyes.

And frankly, it really didn't matter . . . then.

Fast forward to a few months later, when day-to-day realities have made the relationship less dreamy than it felt back then. They are still together, but there are all sorts of those little conflicts emerging and some big ones too. Neither particularly likes the other's children. Both are surprised at how much being "conservative" and "liberal" can influence a person's outlook on life.

And then, the final straw: When Tim moved into Greta's small apartment, he brought Rush Limbaugh with him. And now the man's voice is blaring loudly from the radio in tones Greta is unable to avoid, no matter what room she tries to hide in.

It *does* matter, she suddenly realizes.

Pay Attention

Ironically, the "fatal flaw" that in the end ruins the relationship is usually something that comes out rather early in the dating process . . . and is ignored. Surely if Greta and Tim had not been lost in emotional and hormonal rapture, they would have realized that their different backgrounds, lifestyles, and outlooks on life were bound to create problems down the road.

If you date a man who tells you his lifelong passion is horseback riding and you've never been on a horse, even if he likes the same music you like and is kind and well mannered, he just might not for you.

If you freeze in winter, and your idea of vacation happiness is temperatures in the high eighties, burning sun, and exotic surf, and he tells you he's an avid skier, rather than get excited picturing how handsome he must look in his ski clothes, think about how you will feel freezing there beside him in yours.

If you are a wine lover and he tells you he's a strict teetotaler, rather than respect him for his willpower and healthy lifestyle, think about how you'll feel imbibing solo under a disapproving eye.

If you find yourself dating a guy who always arrives on each date with a very funny anecdote about something terrible that occurred to him that day, it might be a good idea to stop praising his gift as a witty raconteur long enough for a moment of objectivity. Would you have wanted to be there with him when

> The car wouldn't start because he'd forgotten to turn out the interior reading light, and the battery died?
>
> He wasn't paying attention and went the wrong way down a one-way street and almost crashed into a garbage truck?
>
> The cake he'd bought to celebrate a coworker's birthday flipped over, and the icing got all over his clothes?
>
> He completely forgot his sister and her family were coming to stay with him until he found them on his doorstep?

Yes, this man is very funny and gifted with a talent for telling wonderful anecdotes, but what are the personal failings that seem to put him in the middle of these mess-ups?

Many warning signals are ignored in those hopeful, romantic moments that occur at the beginning of a relationship.

Sometimes there is a tendency to ignore the obvious even when he told you so!

Stephanie: I had been out with Jon twice when he brought me home and announced, "No commitments, no expectations," rather abruptly. I was rather surprised and taken aback, wondering what this was all about. In spite of this blunt announcement, our relationship blossomed into one that was comfortable, fun, and satisfying. We skied together, hiked, and shared many common interests. Then one night, he told me he couldn't see me anymore. "I feel as though I'm getting pulled into a vortex with your family and friends," he announced. "It all smacks too much of a commitment." I realized I had been given fair warning but chose to ignore the message. We were able to resume our friendship after a while, but he remains uncommitted to this day (twenty years later), and I suspect he always will.

Sometimes potential conflicts are more difficult to discern right away because there is a difference between what he wants to be and what he is. Self-knowledge, alas, is not a universal virtue. What your date tells you about himself is not necessarily true. We're not saying that the charming man you've just met is a liar. Rather we're saying that there is often a difference between what he says and what he truly feels deep down—a difference that he might not even understand himself.

Andi: Dave was a forty-six-year-old bachelor who told me he really wanted to settle down. He had spent a lot of time searching for Ms. Right, and now was the time to find her and tie the knot. He was looking for a long-term commitment, for marriage, for the works! After we'd been seeing each other for a while, he invited me to his home for dinner. He'd been living in a rental apartment for three years, yet he had not yet unpacked the boxes. Talk about commitment phobic! His plates were paper and his utensils plastic. This was definitely a man who was more interested in being able to make a quick getaway than in settling down.

Neatniks Can Become Noodnicks

Keep in mind that the very characteristics that captivate and fascinate on a date may turn out to be the undoing of a relationship. That's what happened when Julie met Andrew. He took her to his townhouse, which he had decorated beautifully. She really enjoyed listening to him describe all his artwork and how neat he appeared to be. So when he asked her to take off her shoes because his gorgeous floor might get scuffed, she thought nothing about it. Then he asked her not to sit on his white sofa because her dark pants might leave lint. When they got into his sports Mercedes and he asked her not to slam the door, she was getting somewhat annoyed. Then they went to a restaurant and he parked in the middle of two spaces so he wouldn't get dinged. Now here was a man who was interesting and interested in what she had to say, but she knew there was a big problem here. When he brought her home, she slammed the car door and refused to see him again.

Potential Problems

Kammi met Peter on a date. He wasn't at all nice looking but was a well-known successful attorney with his own firm. He made several million dollars a year (as he told her right away), had a gorgeous place in Georgetown, dressed very well, and drove a brand-new Mercedes. He took her to the nicest places. He bragged about the beautiful women he had dated. It was interesting that Peter appeared so cocky, even though he was kind of geeky. They dated for three months, but she never slept with him. She wasn't at all attracted to him but thought things might change when he felt comfortable enough to stop bragging (she attributed his bragging to insecurity). She broke things off after realizing that she wasn't attracted to him, never would be, and she didn't like the kind of person he was. What she saw initially was exactly what she was getting! About a year later, Kammi heard that Peter told a business acquaintance (who happened to be a friend of Kammi's friend) some sick stories of all of the sexual things he did with her! She was outraged knowing that nothing happened. She sent him an e-mail confronting him, and he sent one back admitting that he was wrong, and he was truly sorry for all of the lewd comments and lies he told about her. About six months later, she read in the *Washington Post* that he was arrested for insider trading and fired from his own law firm! Sweet revenge.

Fakai vs. Prell

Andi: Now normally you can't tell much about a man by the kind of shampoo he uses, but I have learned otherwise. I dated Bob, the Prell guy, for three months. He was nice enough but a bit on the bland side. He preferred staying home and making dinner, serving Wishbone Russian Dressing (I thought it was discontinued years ago). I felt like we were a married couple—we'd go out, come home and go to sleep, he on his side and me on mine. He went to bed fully clothed in sweatpants and a sweatshirt. He was unaffectionate, quiet, and had few interests. So what was I doing with him? He was kind and nice, and I had nothing else going on in my life. Then Joey appeared, a seemingly successful attorney, who wooed me from the first date, though I told him I was seeing someone else. Joey asked about him, and when I told him that Bob was a doctor, he replied, "You've got the Jewish woman's classic dilemma. "Will it be the doctor or the lawyer?" He pursued me ardently, writing poems, and calling and text messaging regularly. Though he lived in Philadelphia, he often had business in Washington. I saw him one weekend when Bob wasn't available and found him very appealing. In short, he had the joie de vivre that Bob was missing. Oh, did I mention he also used Fakai shampoo, a bit more exciting than Prell? I ended my relationship with Bob (in a nice way, of course) and began seeing Joey. Talk about wining and dining! We went away for a fabulous weekend. He bought me an expensive necklace after just a month together. Things were looking great. So far, what I saw was what I was getting, and it was all good. I invited Joey for the weekend and invited my sister and brother-in-law for dinner. Two days later, my brother-in-law called, telling me that Joey had been fired from his law firm for sexual harassment and that he had cheated on both of his ex-wives. He was known for dumping women when the next best thing showed up. Then I found out he owed the IRS $500,000! I tried to return the necklace he gave me, but he wouldn't take it. What a disappointment he turned out to be! So much for what you see is what you'll get.

Less Obvious Potential Problems

We all know that a date puts his best foot forward at the beginning, and that is the basis for our first impression. Some people can keep the charm on for a few months, but you can only playact for so long. If the charm is a put-on rather than something intrinsic to his personality, sooner or later the wolf in sheep's clothing emerges. Time is what it takes to help you discern this.

We think it's important to give a promising relationship at least a year to let the flaws appear. During that time, you'll not only want to remain alert and discerning; you'll want to meet his family and close friends. How do they interact? Does he have a solid relationship with his parents and siblings? If he has children, is he a good father? How do his friends view him, and are his friends the kind of people you would want as your friends? If not, why not?

What is his rationale for important decisions? Does it make sense to you? You need your investigator skills to read into what he says and how he says it. It's okay to be a little skeptical in the beginning. A partner needs to earn your trust. As you get to know him over time and see him in various situations, you can let your guard down. This will save you a lot of embarrassment and hurt because there are a lot of bad seeds out there, and finding Mr. Right takes a lot of effort and time. We don't want you to get discouraged and think this is not what you bargained for. There truly is someone out there for everyone. You just want to make sure the one you find will be a long-term keeper.

And while you are analyzing and looking for signals, here are some types to reconsider:

Mr. Needy. Needy men have a certain Montgomery Clift-like appeal. It is very satisfying to be told, for example, that *only you* can make him laugh in a way that brings him out of his depressive state. *Only you* can cook the kind of food he wants to eat. *Only you* are the understanding listener he has craved for so long. *Only you* can bring him out of his shell.

What, however, do you do when you lose this unique capability, when, say, try as you may to be funny, he lingers in his depressive state?

And even if your magical charm manages to stay with you, being a savior can get tiring. How many at-your-house meals will you have to prepare for the man who only wants to eat your cooking?

How long will it take you to realize that being an understanding listener is a passive role that never enables you to have an audience of your own?

And when he tells you lovingly that he's never known someone as contagiously warm, outgoing, and social as you because, to tell the truth, he's always been a bit of a loner, without any close friends to speak of . . . you might want to take a "time-out" and have a private conversation with yourself.

Sure, it's exciting to be the one to "bring him out of the isolation he's existed in for the last twenty years," but twenty years is a long time. CAN you bring him out? Will someone as extroverted as you are be happy sitting alone with him in his cave when he retreats to the past behavior that he finds comfortable?

Now, we're not saying get rid of the needy ones. We're just saying that time works miracles. Give those relationships time. See how well the neediness ages before committing.

The Blamer. This is the man who has had the bad luck to go through life doing his best, trying his hardest, leading an exemplary existence, only to have *other people* rob him of the credit/fortune/joy/success/accomplishments/tranquility/love he needs and deserves. People who blame others on a regular basis generally aren't willing to take responsibility for their actions. Soon he will be blaming you for his problems.

Mr. "If Only." This is a variation of the blamer who blames situations rather than individuals. *If only* he'd managed to get his idea to the patent office first, he'd be a wealthy man now. *If only* he'd taken the other job, his life wouldn't be such a mess. Too many *if onlys* can be signs of someone who is stuck in a situation and unable to move on. Sure, we all deal with disappointments in life, and it's healthy to express those disappointments. After a time, however, it's time to turn your focus to future accomplishments.

The Cheapskate. He is never hungry and only too willing to "share a meal" when he takes you out to a restaurant, but suddenly famished when you are doing the cooking. He would rather stay at home and "gaze into your beautiful eyes" than take in a movie, play, sports event, or, to be blunt, do anything that costs money.

Find out more about his financial situation. Gloria dated a tall, dark, handsome man with whom she had great chemistry and with whom she had a lot of fun. The only thing wrong with him was an enormous reluctance to spend money. She later found out he owed a fortune to the IRS, was deep into credit card debt, and was in the throes of a nasty divorce with huge legal fees.

Mr. Phi Beta Kappa. Brilliance is a totally positive attribute, so long as the person who is fortunate enough to embody it is not too caught up in himself. The ingenious scientific researcher might make for fascinating listening the first few dates, but after a while the charm wears off as you realize you are just a receptacle, and, sad to tell, he is more enamored with himself than you are with him. (The *truly* brilliant are perceptive enough to know that they need to know as much as possible about their date, and therefore are as requesting of information as they are giving it.)

Calvin Critical. The food is too cold, the weather too warm, the children too indulged, the traffic awful as usual. The movie was dreary, the concert amateur fare. Why is the car always messy? That dress is kind of loud, don't you think? Blue is not a good color for you, and that entrée you chose is filled with cholesterol. Is that your second glass of wine? (Our feeling: There are enough clouds in everyday life without consciously inviting one to be your partner!)

The Smoothie. He brings you flowers. He holds open doors. He is so extremely attentive it feels a little . . . overly attentive. He wines and dines you and compliments you and . . . could this be too good to be true?

Andi: Carl was charming plus! After the first date, he sent me a box of assorted coffees because he knew I had to get up early every day, and coffee helped me get started. My every wish was his command, it seemed. I referred to him as the "perfect peach." Well, the perfect peach soon turned into the "rotten apple" when I heard he had taken out someone else and sent her a bouquet of flowers after their first date. Then the rumors began that he had been an abusive husband, had a bad temper, and that he always came on strong and then vanished. Be on the alert when things seem too perfect.

What should you do when the flaws appear? (And they surely will. Even the good ones have flaws.) Do you end the relationship?

Of course not. You step back and evaluate the flaw. Is it one you can overlook, given all the other winning characteristics he has going for him? Or is it of the "fatal flaw" variety? How important is it?

Will it adversely affect your relationship?

Could you learn to accept it if everything else is good?

Forget About Changing Him

Accept is what we're talking about here—accept rather than change. Many people go into relationships thinking they can change the person, only to realize how deeply entrenched behavior can be.

We're not saying he can't change; we're saying your goal might not be his goal, and he has to *want* to change enough to invest time and energy into working at it. Think of all the years of habit that went before you. Contemplate how built into his character the part of him you want to change might be. Ask yourself whether he is open to feedback. Some people just can't take criticism, no matter how gentle!

Take Your Time!

Fatal flaws don't always appear right away. Sonia met William through Match.com. He was a successful attorney who was ten years older than she was. He was very active, going on international bike tours and scuba diving in Belize. He was bright and interesting, dressed impeccably, and knew how to treat a woman, or so it seemed. Their first two dates went very well; the conversation flowed easily, and there appeared to be mutual chemistry. On the third date, Sonia noticed he had started correcting her grammar and questioning her facts when she told him an anecdote. On the fifth date, he seemed even more supercilious, voicing strong opinions on everything from child rearing to why marriages break up. On the sixth date, he told her he couldn't stand her gum-chewing and she said "amazing" too much. By the eighth date, Sonia felt as though she were walking on eggshells. She couldn't wait until the evening was over.

William had transformed himself before her eyes from a warm, friendly, and interesting man to an arrogant, judgmental, and critical one. It had taken a number of dates for his true self to shine through.

Sometimes You Never Know

Jennifer met Bryan on Match.com. He had a nice profile and posted pictures of himself with his three children. It turned out they had a mutual friend who assured Jennifer he came from a nice family. They dated for six months, and things were going great. He was attentive, funny, engaging, a great father, and a true pleasure to be with. One night when he was sleeping at her home, she became very sick, vomiting several times. She slept on the couch, so she wouldn't disturb him. The next morning he asked where she was all night, and she explained how sick she was. He left telling her to feel better. She never heard from him again! Not a single message or e-mail! After a few weeks, she wanted to call him but talked to their mutual friend first. Bryan's sister-in-law confided to her that Bryan had serious anger-management problems. When his ex-girlfriend provoked him, he tried to strangle her with a scarf! She also heard that his ex-wife was terrified of him and slept with a gun under her bed! She couldn't believe it, but it was confirmed by another person who had known him for years. Egads! She spent six months with the guy and never had a clue. Was she glad she hadn't pissed him off!

There is Such a Thing as a Happy Ending!

Yes, there are some horror stories out there that may turn you off the dating scene. Sadly, the ones in this book are all true, but they are but a tiny fraction of the multitude of normal, happy people and couples. A couple recently interviewed on a morning talk show were celebrating their sixty-fifth wedding anniversary. "What's the secret?" the interviewer asked. The husband replied, "Have fun, laugh a lot, respect each other, and don't give her any lip." Works for them!

Look at your friends and family in long-term relationships and marriages. Are these marriages perfect? Of course not, but these couples have worked through problems, either alone, or with professional help, because they knew they had something good and were willing to do what it took to get things on the right path again. They learned how to communicate, how to let their partner know when something was wrong. They were able to talk about negative feelings instead of stuffing them. What they saw initially was still there, even through life's ups and downs. So don't let a few rotten apples prevent you from finding happiness with the right partner.

Dos and Don'ts of
What You See and Hear isn't Always What You'll Get

Do

- Trust your instincts.
- Listen carefully to what he tells you about himself.
- Be observant. The old adage that actions often speak louder than words contains a lot of truth.
- Get as much information about him as you can.
- Be patient. Sometimes it takes a long time to realize that what you saw initially isn't what is. Character flaws may take a long time to reveal themselves.

Don't

- Stay in a bad relationship hoping things will improve. They're usually the best at the beginning.
- Rush things; there's plenty of time to decide if this is a solid relationship.
- Fool yourself about his intentions. If you think he's not being up front about who he is, get rid of him.
- Waste your time when you know in your heart that he's not for you.
- Bank on changing him. Some things can be changed, others cannot.

Chapter Ten

How do We Handle the Children?

☹ No one wants to date a woman with two girls, one boy, a cat, and four goldfish.

☹ As a single working mom, I have no time to date.

☹ For the children's sake, I need to dedicate all my time to them.

Wrong on all counts! Adult companionship is essential from time to time, and romance is a huge adrenalin shot. If you're sacrificing your social life for your children, you are not doing them any favor. You need to take care of your own emotional, social, and physical needs in order to be upbeat enough to handle theirs. And while you might have trouble finding someone who can develop an emotional attachment to four goldfish, there are many men out there who like children and want to date someone with children.

This is your decision. You do not need your children's approval to date, and, in fact, if you seek their approval you are giving them too much control. You don't want to do that. You are the adult in this relationship. You make the decisions. If you feel ready for a social life and act confident about your decision to go out on dates, your children will accept it and eventually respect it.

Be open about it. Explain to your children that just as they like to have friends their own age to play with, you need friends your age. In the same way, be up front with your date on the importance of your children in your life. Make sure your date knows that you are a package deal. "Postponing" telling someone that you are a parent as well as a person is not the way to begin a relationship!

Talk things out.

Stephanie: When I told my children I was going on my first date, the response was varied. Gary, age fifteen, said, "Be home by twelve." Susan, age seventeen, said, "No kissing," and Andi, age thirteen, said, "Already?"

It's common for children to have different reactions to a parent's dating and important to hear them out. If your husband has died, his memory will be very important to your children, and they may worry you are trying to replace him with someone else—a stranger. It's important to allow them to express these concerns and assure them Dad will always occupy an enduring place in their lives, that no one could ever replace their father. Encourage your children to talk about their feelings, and when they tell you what you don't want to hear, assure them that you understand. Remember, there's a difference between understanding feelings and agreeing with them. Don't let yourself be bullied.

If you are divorced, your dating may at first feel threatening to your children because they are still secretly entertaining the hope that you and their father will reunite.

Andi: I had been divorced for a while when my seven-year-old said to me, "I want to spend time with you and Dad, together." I was so taken aback but then realized this was an opportunity to talk to her about our divorce, and the fact that we were both dating other people. Our conversation went as follows:

Me: I know it must be hard for you that Daddy and I aren't together.

Nicole: I dunno.

Me: Well, you said you wished you could spend time with both of us together.

Nicole: Yeah.

Me: Can you tell me a little more about what you were thinking?

Nicole: I can't remember.

Me: Well, how does it feel when you go places with Daddy and his lady friend, and Mommy isn't there?

Nicole: Fine. We had such a fun time when we went to the Renaissance Festival, and Daddy bought me a bracelet!

I decided that we would revisit this topic some other time. One thing I've learned is you can't push kids to talk about their feelings; rather the topic has to be gently coaxed out of them when they are ready.

Preparing for Dating

Yes, you're going to need *childcare*. In order to date you will, of course, need babysitters if you have young children, adequate supervision when you're not there if you have older children. (Many women arrange dates for when their former spouses have the children for the weekend.)

Yes, your *balancing act* will become even more off balance. You wondered before how you could divide twenty-four hours into so many parts, all needing your attention, and now here you go adding an extra part. This extra part might provide a good excuse for teaching your children to do more around the house so you can do a little less. Even young children can learn to fold clothes, fill and empty the dishwasher, and put away groceries. They learn quickly and can do much more than we think.

Yes, there will be *guilt*. (You are a mother after all.) Shouldn't you be home supervising the multiplication tables? Are the teenagers you left home doing something they shouldn't be doing? Cell phones are a necessity for dating mothers—to stay in touch and to be reachable.

Yes, your *child will react*. A lot depends on your child's age. Older children, who are attempting to deal with their own emerging sexuality, may be embarrassed to have a mother who is also dating. It's sometimes difficult for younger children when there are changes in routines, like a mother suddenly getting dressed up and going out. Watch them for signals, and whenever possible, encourage them to talk about their feelings.

Where do I Look for a Date?

The places suggested in chapter 7 should give you many ideas, but if you are a single mother looking for a single father you might also look around when you take your children to places other parents and children frequent. Playgrounds are for children, granted, but little children are taken there by their parents—many of whom are single.

You probably never have thought of a zoo or a children's museum as a good place to "meet men," but the truth is, meeting people when you are with your children is often easier than when you're alone. They are great conversation starters, especially with men who have children the same age.

Getting Ready to Go Out

So much depends on how old your children are. If you have toddlers, of course, there is no need to explain where you are going or why when you go out on a date.

For children old enough to understand, explain that you are going out with a friend. Make sure young children know you are not dating because you don't like spending time with them but because everyone needs to spend time with people their own age.

For older children, it's best to downplay the importance of what you are about to do, and be especially attentive for reactions. The older they are, the better they are at camouflage, and the wider variety of reactions they might have.

Andi: Four years after my divorce, my twelve-year-old came to me crying out of the blue that he didn't want me to date anyone, and he didn't want his dad to either. He had seemed happy and content for the past four years, so I was surprised when he said this. I gave him positive encouragement for discussing his feelings and told him how important that was. I realized that he had been holding all of his sadness about the divorce inside, and I felt guilty that I had been so busy trying to juggle my life that I was completely unaware that he had all of these sad feelings.

My daughter on the other hand loves to go searching for men for me on Match.com and loves reading the profiles! I was dating someone for about two months, and she kept saying that I needed a backup plan in case things didn't work out.

Even if your children are grown and out of the house, when you decide to date, you need to have a conversation with the kids. There may be some surprises here. You think they'll be so happy that Mom will be happy, that Mom will be less dependent on them, but it ain't necessarily so. Some adult children prefer the status quo with Mom being Mom—available to babysit and there whenever needed. Others may have concerns about their inheritance.

Meet your first date in places away from your home.

Make sure your actions match your words. If you tell your child you will be back from your date before he or she goes to bed, be sure to get home on time.

When you're out with someone, leave home behind. Don't sabotage the potential relationship at its very beginning by compensating for your mixed feelings about leaving your children behind by talking about them endlessly. Everyone needs to spend time with people their own age, you told your child. So do just that. Enjoy the adult company.

Don't introduce your children to a date until the relationship has matured and you really know him and feel this could be serious. It doesn't matter whether they are five or fifteen, children don't have the maturity to understand the adult dating world. The last thing your children need is to meet men who come by once or twice and then are gone for good. Realize that if your children grow attached to someone who ends up walking out on you and them, they are likely to feel the same hurt or pain when the relationship breaks off that you feel. Protect them. Keep your dates to yourself until you find one that matters.

Your children are not appropriate confidants about dating relationship issues. Don't add to their confusion by offering too much information.

When You Have Found Someone Special

Take care not to get so carried away you forget priorities. Helping with the science project might be less fun than a romantic evening but more necessary for family health.

When you decide it's time—that this "date" is more than a date, and you want him to meet your young children—avoid making him the centerpiece, and avoid adult activity like dinner in a restaurant. The first meeting should be casual, like having him pick you up at home a half hour early so he can spend a short amount of time saying hi to your kids. Or you might arrange the first meeting around something your children enjoy doing—ice skating or a trip to the swimming pool or a picnic at the zoo—some activity where they will be comfortable and somewhat preoccupied.

Be careful about displaying affection in front of them. No matter how old they are, they know more but understand less than you might think.

Expect some resistance. You might bring a perfectly nice man home for a visit, and your children will act out, especially if this is the first time you've been serious about someone other than their father. And be prepared. Adult children will be more subtle than young children, but they can be just as hurtful.

The Deal Breakers

Andi: I met a really nice man who had three children with ages similar to mine. After we'd been dating for a while, I invited his children to brunch. While two of them were sweet and kind, the third one was a monster. She was sullen, nasty, and obviously didn't want to be at my home. I could see how manipulative she was. Had Bruce taken a tough stand with her, I would have been able to handle things better. I decided on a wait-and-watch approach. But the more time we spent together, the nastier she got; and instead of disciplining her, he kept mollifying her. My children didn't like her and neither did I. It was time to end the relationship. So this controlling twelve-year-old won again because her father felt too guilty to put her in her place.

When you are in a relationship and there are children involved, you can't assume things will work out in time. The truth is no situation has more deal-breaking variables than dating with children. You might hate his. He might hate yours. His children might not get along with yours, or yours might be uncomfortable with his. He might not have children and be jealous of the relationship between you and yours. He might begin disciplining yours in ways you don't like. He may parent his own children in ways you don't respect.

There are compromises that can be made if everything else in the relationship is good. It's important to investigate what is behind the "not liking" and see if it is a legitimate gripe. Children are, after all, unfinished products. They change and grow and as they do, their feelings may change.

Each step of a dating relationship necessitates a "pulse-taking" talk with the children. Talk to yourself, too. Ask yourself how important this or that problem really is. If your answer is "big," it may be time to reevaluate this relationship.

Talk things out with him in detail too. How much family time will you spend together? How will you work his kids in the equation? How will you handle big age differences? How much involvement does he really want in your kids' lives, especially if his are much older? Will that be enough for you? Remember, you and your children are a package. If you're a parent who is deeply involved with your kids' activities, how will you feel if he only wants to have a peripheral role? These are complex questions—not easy to answer—but ones that must be brought up.

And then finally, there is the flip side: Your children are crazy about him, but you are becoming less and less enamored. Bear in mind that change is a part of life. Hard as it may be to break up with someone your kids have become attached to, if you realize it's not going to work as far as you are concerned, break up with him. Staying together for the sake of the offspring makes even less sense when you're not married! This can be a learning experience for all of you.

Do's and Don'ts of Dating with Children

Do

- Remember that it's okay to take time-out for yourself.
- Encourage your children to discuss their feelings.

- Seek professional help or group therapy for your child if a problem persists. (Group therapy for children of divorced parents really helped Andi's daughter, Nicole, to hear how other kids felt about their parents' divorces.)
- Try to spend private quality time with each child even if only for a short time.
- Keep all information age appropriate.
- Be up front and honest, gentle, but firm.

Don't

- Promise them that you are not going to date. Be truthful but understand where they are coming from.
- Introduce them to your dates too soon. Too many are fleeting!
- Rush things; let them take their own course.
- Allow your children to manipulate you. When you're ready to date, tell them and don't back down because of their unhappiness.
- Pretend that the problems with the children (his or yours) don't matter and will work out eventually. They need to be dealt with.

Chapter Eleven

Lighten Up!

Karen was very attractive and bright, a divorcee, in her late thirties who was desperate to put her terrible marriage behind her by finding someone new and wonderful who would be the right partner for the rest of her life. Her experience thus far—both in marriage and in online dating—had been negative enough to make her highly suspicious of just about every male who answered her e-mails.

Sam was in his late thirties and so fed up with Match.com he contemplated trashing his computer. Internet dating thus far had brought a slew of awful women into his life. Either they had cruelly rejected him or turned out to be horribly demanding or even downright insane. Several, in fact, he would place into that last category. But Karen's pictures were attractive, and her e-mails were both intelligent and fun to answer.

Karen felt the same way about Sam. She had started looking forward to his e-mails each night and to the challenge of thinking up clever responses.

After a few weeks, Sam suggested they meet at a nearby bar for a glass of wine.

Karen hated bars, especially the one Sam had suggested, which was noisy, unattractive, and filled with twenty- and thirty-something singles looking to mate. Karen suggested instead that Sam just come by her apartment for a glass of wine.

Sam balked. "What's wrong with the bar?"

Karen raised an eyebrow. "What's wrong with my apartment?" she e-mailed back.

"Is there a reason you don't want to go out?" Sam replied, sounding suddenly suspicious.

"Are you afraid of my apartment?" Karen retorted, confused by the hostile tone she had noted in Sam's latest e-mail. "Maybe we should just forget the whole thing!"

"No, fine. Okay. Your apartment," he e-mailed back.

Her hopes went down the drain. This one was going to turn out like all the others.

The first few minutes after his arrival were awkward. He seemed edgy to her. He kept looking around nervously and for some reason sneaking glances at her feet. She wondered whether meeting him in a public place would have been smarter. Was he going to turn out to be the Boston Strangler?

He took a sip of wine and clenched his jaw. "Why did you want to meet here?" he asked sternly.

She shrugged. "Why not?"

"Are you allowed to go out?"

Her heart beat faster. This was definitely a kook. "Of course," she said sarcastically, "I'm thirty-six. I'm allowed to do whatever I want to do!"

"Sorry. Sorry. I just had a bad experience before."

"With an Internet date?"

Sam nodded.

"An Internet date who invited you to her place?"

He nodded again.

She was almost afraid to ask. "What happened?"

"Nothing. It's just . . . well it turned out, she, um, had to stay home. Couldn't go out."

Karen shook her head, totally confused. "Why?"

"Well, uh, because she was under house arrest."

Karen's jaw dropped. "What?"

Sam nodded soberly. "She'd robbed a store. The Dade County Sherriff's office had put an electronic device on her ankle to monitor where she was at all times . . . to, um, make sure she stayed home."

Karen felt the laughter building, building inside her until finally she could control it no more. "A robber winked at you on match-dot-com?" she shouted, exploding into giggles. "Your perfect match turned out to be a convict!"

Sam started to speak, but her giggling was contagious. He suddenly realized it was funny. He began laughing so hard he had to put the glass down to keep the wine from spilling. "She wrote great e-mails!" he blurted out.

"Well, she had extra time to practice!"

The two howled even louder.

That is a true story. Karen and Sam did eventually manage to find true love and live "happily ever after"—although it was with two other people, not with each other. But that evening they forged a friendship that continues today.

The anecdote is significant because it underscores several important principles of dating.

One is, you never know whom you are going to meet on the Internet, or even when you are fixed up by mutual friends. *A thief under house arrest?* There are most certainly some weirdos out there. You need to be careful, watchful, and protective; but if you are, although you will probably encounter some annoying people, no harm will come to you. There is nothing to be afraid of.

Another principle is beware of cynicism. It only takes a few bad dates before you begin rejecting possibilities instinctively, suspecting the worst of everyone who crosses your path—either because you are worrying about rejection or because you are worrying about getting stuck for another evening with a dork. It's *his* loss if he rejects you, and what's so terrible about one date with a dork (especially if you are compensated by seeing a good movie or going to a nice restaurant in the process)?

The real lesson of this story, however, is that lightening up a little—taking things less seriously—is essential to dating successfully. Too often people approach "finding Mr. Right" as a chore, a job, something that must be accomplished in a select time period—or else.

Dating, we feel, should be an experience in and of itself, as well as a means to an end. It should be fun, interesting, an adventure.

Relax a little. Stop worrying that you are wasting time with a loser, or that you don't look as good as you'd hoped, or that you could never fall for this type of guy, or that this type of guy could never fall for you. Concentrate instead on doing whatever it takes to have a good time. Laugh a little. Did you know laughing actually lowers the levels of stress hormones circulating in your blood? That's one good reason to laugh right there! But there are other reasons. Laugh and if your date laughs with you—the way Sam laughed with Karen—he will *connect* with you. When you laugh at the same thing, after all, your brains are in sync. You are emotionally tuning in to one another.

Are you having trouble finding something to laugh about? Then try putting yourself in a better mood by smiling. Studies show that the facial muscles involved in the sheer act of smiling trigger positive impulses to the brain by increasing endorphins. Smiling, therefore, all by itself is joy enhancing.

So smile, relax, and give him a chance. And while you're at it, bear in mind the importance of timing.

Bonny was a seventy-nine-year-old widow, and for her the timing was perfect. She had heard wonderful things about Nathan, an eighty-five-year-old widower who had lost his wife a month after she lost her husband. About a year later, friends suggested they meet, but she wasn't ready. Then she heard he had met Alice, a woman she knew, and was seeing her exclusively. Two years later Alice died. When her friends asked her if they could give Nathan her name, she said yes. The timing was right for both of them. He called and invited her for lunch, showing up in tennis shoes and jeans, which was a bit off-putting (she was expecting lunch at the Ritz). In spite of that, they hit it off right away. He called her soon after, and they've been together ever since. They live apart but spend nights and weekends together. They've now been together for three years and are deliciously happy. When they were first together, Nathan would sometimes call Bonny, Barbie, his first wife's name. One night she appeared in a T-shirt saying, "I'm Bonny." "We laugh all the time," Bonny said. Our friends call us the "Cute Couple." "Who would have thought we could find happiness at our ages?"

Timing is crucial at any age. When Lacey met Frank at a mutual friend's party, Lacey, thirty-eight, was with her boyfriend, and Frank, thirty-one, was with his girlfriend. Neither relationship was going well. Shortly after the party, Frank decided it was over. Lacey, too, had been with her boyfriend for five years but determined it was going nowhere and ended it. Frank and Lacey reconnected at a mutual friend's wedding (thank God for mutual friends) a few weeks later. They started hanging out together. Both had certain expectations of each other based on their previous long-term relationships. While they enjoyed being together, there were lots of ups and downs; Frank, especially, had strong ideas of how things should be. She found him somewhat uptight, easily stressed, and a strong type A person. He was very direct and honest—often to a fault. He felt she thought too much before speaking. She felt she simply measured her words carefully. After a year, she decided she'd rather be his friend; and he agreed, but they rarely saw each other.

After a couple of months, she called him to meet for a drink. She drove to his house in an ice storm and was stuck overnight. They reevaluated their relationship and decided to give it another go. There were strong feelings on both sides, and things took off. Now they're able to talk about issues they see differently. They are both more open about their feelings. She's working on being more spontaneous, and he's working on being less spontaneous! They have moved in together and are discussing marriage. Frank is working on being more mellow and relaxed. Lacey is learning to lighten up and not be so serious. She agrees that life is filled with surprises, and many turn out to be good ones.

We have had lots of good dates and lots of bad ones. It is important to go in with reasonable expectations so you won't be disappointed. Mr. Right could very well turn out to be Mr. Wrong. But it is even more important to go in with a positive attitude. There is something redeeming in almost everyone. You just have to find it, not because it will convince you to spend the rest of your life with him. Rather because it will make the rest of your evening together more enjoyable.

Lest you think we, the authors, don't practice what we preach, we would like to end this book with an update on our current status.

Andi: I met Thierry one and a half years ago at a local supermarket. He recognized me because we used to take our kids to the same school bus stop. We began chatting, and it turned out we used to live around the corner from each other. I found him attractive, with a sexy French accent. It turns out he, too, was divorced with three children. He invited me out to dinner to a new French bistro. Have you ever had an evening when everything was perfect? It was a beautiful evening, and he couldn't have been more charming. We talked for five hours! You could say it was true chemistry. And so began a relationship unlike any other I had experienced. He loved art, music, cooking, and his family. We went to art galleries and museums and did so many interesting things together. He continued to invite me out, and there was no game playing. He told me he wanted a solid relationship and wasn't interested in dating around. It was exactly what I wanted to hear, but of course, I was guarded based on my past experiences. In time I saw that he was a man of his word. I became more trusting and found myself falling in love. Thierry is intelligent, attractive, and appealing. He's a loving and devoted father with three warm and friendly children. We started getting together with our families and were thrilled that the kids got along so well. We traveled to France where he introduced me to his family, showed me Paris, and took me skiing in the French Alps. It was breathtaking. We ate wonderful food, delicious pastries, and delicacies and drank chilled French champagne. The three pounds I gained in that week were worth it; it was the most incredible trip I have taken.

I was intrigued by all the cultural differences, though at times some of them became pronounced and challenging. We had two breakups, mostly due to our cultural differences, but we were able to work through them. We talked openly and honestly at a deep level, which was difficult and painful, but now our relationship is stronger than ever. This is the first mature relationship I have had since my marriage, and it feels so right. I have found the perfect person for me, and it is nice that my search for Mr. Right is officially over. I think that the five years of dating did help me understand what I wanted and needed, and if I had met Thierry right after my divorce, it probably wouldn't have worked. I believe in that timeworn cliché that timing is everything, and you have to kiss a lot of toads before you meet your handsome prince. Many people told me, "When it is right, you will know it." I know I have found my lifetime mate, and it has been the most wonderful period in my life.

Stephanie: I never expected to marry again. I had been widowed after nineteen years and divorced after six. During the next ten years, I developed a good life with lots of friends, a wonderful career, and many interests. I dated many men but hadn't yet met "the one," and it was truly okay. Then I met Lee. I remember the first time he called. It was the night of the Bloomingdale's sale, and my grandchildren were staying over. There was a huge thunderstorm, and my grandson begged me not to go to Bloomies. I agreed to stay home, and lo and behold, the phone rang and it was Lee. A mutual friend had given him my phone number. He lived in Atlantic City, and I lived in Maryland, though I had grown up in Atlantic City. "Where have you been for the past forty years?" I asked, jokingly.

He had found out I was planning to be in Atlantic City for the July 4 weekend and called in hopes of setting up a date.

We met, and there was instant rapport. When he said goodnight, he said, "Well, there's certainly chemistry between us, but you live in Maryland, and I live here."

"And you have a car, and I have a car," I replied, "so I don't see a problem."

And there wasn't. We had a long-distance relationship for three years, traveling together, and spending weekends at each other's homes, and life was grand. Soon, the prospect of marriage seemed right for both of us. I was sixty-three, and Lee was sixty-eight. We had six children between us and nine grandchildren at the time of our wedding (we now have ten). Mine are crazy about Lee, and I hope his children feel the same way about me.

We married on July 4, 2003, exactly three years after the day we met. I know I speak for him when I say we are so happy, that we have found our soul mates.

What makes our marriage work so well, in addition to loving each other, is humor. If I get upset about some trivial thing, he makes a joke out of it, and soon we're both laughing. We laugh a lot. We rely on each other's strengths and understand and accept each other's weaknesses. We tend to hug a lot—at the beginning and end of each day and in-between, as well. Sometimes, we think the same thoughts and finish each other's sentences. Scary!

I'm a type A person, and Lee knows how to keep me calm (or at least calmer). If I get annoyed I ask myself, "In the scheme of things, how important is this?" The answer usually is not at all. We are able to discuss issues, even delicate ones, so we don't store up resentment and let things simmer.

For Lee, getting married meant retiring from his medical practice and moving to Maryland, not an easy feat after spending most of his life in Atlantic City. My friends became his friends, and he adjusted to life very well. We can't believe how lucky we are to have found each other at this stage in our lives.

My advice to single women seeking a relationship is to hang in there; love can happen at any age. Spend time doing the things you enjoy doing so finding a man doesn't become your sole purpose in life. Use your resources to create a satisfying and sustaining life. And don't forget to let friends and acquaintances know you'd like to meet someone—it's important to advertise!

We wish all of our readers happiness, hope, and humor as they pursue a meaningful and enduring relationship.